Waterskiing

Waterskiing

Kenneth Stephens
With the assistance of John Flowers

McGraw-Hill Ryerson Limited

Toronto   Montreal   New York   London   Sydney
Johannesburg   Mexico   Panama   Düsseldorf
Singapore   São Paulo   Kuala Lumpur
New Delhi

Waterskiing

Copyright © McGraw-Hill Ryerson Limited, 1974.
All rights reserved. No part of this publication may be reproduced, stored in a retrieval system, or transmitted in any form or by any means, electronic, mechanical, photocopying, recording, or otherwise, without the prior written permission of McGraw-Hill Ryerson Limited.

Photography by Barry Ranford, except for pages 77 (center photo), 88 (right photo), 112, 113 (left photo), 116, 119 and 121 copyright photographs by Hans P. Gulde taken at the MOLSON'S water ski show, courtesy MOLSON'S BREWERY.

Diagrams by W. E. Ruck.

ISBN 0-07-077762-4

Library of Congress Catalog Card Number 74-11780

2 3 4 5 6 7 8 9 10   D   4 3 2 1 0 9 8 7 6 5

Printed and bound in Canada

To Ellis and Marg
For their continuous encouragement

Acknowledgements

The author wishes to acknowledge the assistance of the following companies/associations in the preparation of this book:

1. American Water Ski Association
2. Bangor Lodge Limited
3. Canadian Water Ski Association—Ontario Region
4. John Leckie Limited
5. Margesson and Company Limited
6. Mercury Marine Limited
7. O'Brien Water Skis
8. Raven Lake Cottagers' Association
9. Sea Gliders Skis
10. The Fitness Institute

And the following persons:

Mr. Craig Baxter, Mr. David Bournes, Mr. Don Brett, Dr. John Flowers, Mr. James Harper, Mr. Peter Herbert, Miss Leslie Hood, Mr. Rick Humble, Mr. Dave Northcote, Mr. Paul Roberts, Mrs. Joan Scott, Mr. Grant Tadman, Mr. Don West, and Miss Barbara Wright.

Contents

Preface

Chapter	1	Safety in Waterskiing	11
Chapter	2	Ski Boats and Driving	17
Chapter	3	Beginner Two Ski	26
Chapter	4	Beginner One Ski	38
Chapter	5	Slalom Skiing	46
Chapter	6	Jumping	56
Chapter	7	Trick Skiing	66
Chapter	8	Barefoot Skiing	84
Chapter	9	Kite Skiing	92
Chapter	10	Show Skiing	106
Chapter	11	Conditioning	122
Chapter	12	Equipment Maintenance	136

Preface

This book was prepared primarily as a guideline for the recreational waterskier. Its purpose, while initiating some thoughts on safety, is to raise the skill level of the average waterskier and increase his enjoyment of the sport.

However, there is another reason for writing this book. It is my opinion that one way of advancing the knowledge and techniques involved in any sport is for someone to set down their concepts or ideas so that others might subject them to test and possibly improve upon them. I have set down the methods for learning how to waterski which I believe to be the most successful and the easiest to follow. It is up to you to test them and make the necessary changes.

To any instructor utilizing the book, have the basics before you. Adapt this material to your own teaching style. Be flexible—implement your own methods to build on the base established here. Ask yourself how you can present the material to the student before you. Remember, a good instructor exudes confidence and knowledge, and instills the same in a novice.

Very little mention of the competitive aspects of the sport has been made in the book. Competitive waterskiing is exciting, physically demanding, and extremely rewarding. However, the best way to become a competitive waterskier is to join an association. You will receive the instruction and coaching necessary for tournament skiing.

Acknowledgement should be made of several special contributions. The staff of Summer Water Ski Services, one of the best show skiing troops in North America, provided the fine skiing illustrated throughout the book. The advice of Mr. Grant Tadman on conditioning and Mr. Craig Baxter's photography of the conditioning sequences add immensely to the book. Invaluable criticism and instruction was given the author by Mr. Peter Herbert, Mr. Don West and Mr. Paul Roberts. In addition, the contributions of Mr. James Harper and Dr. John Flowers were immeasurable. Mr. Harper has advanced the quality of waterski instruction markedly, and many of his views are reflected here. Without the encouragement and technical assistance given by Dr. Flowers, this book might never have been finished.

Kenneth E. Stephens

Chapter 1 Safety in Waterskiing

Waterskiing is an enjoyable and immensely exciting sport as well as a mentally and physically demanding one. The skier who acknowledges the risk of personal danger and takes steps to avoid the occurrence of accidents is the person who is most likely to experience full enjoyment of the sport.

Often the beginner, in his enthusiasm to get on the water, overlooks the importance of safety in waterskiing. Adherence to safety procedures is the key to prolonged enjoyment of waterskiing. Those interested in taking up the sport must take the time to familiarize themselves with safety procedures.

ARTIFICIAL RESPIRATION

Anyone who participates in a water sport should be able to perform mouth-to-mouth artificial respiration. (Full courses in artificial respiration and water safety are available from the local branch of the Red Cross Society.)

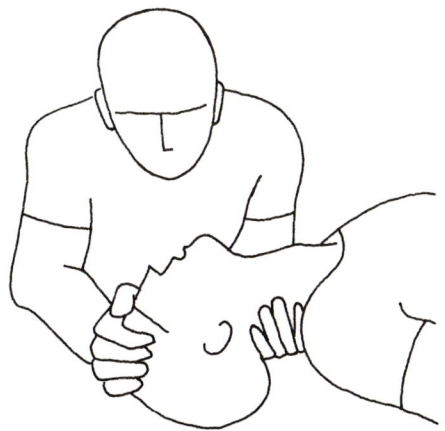

How to give mouth-to-mouth artificial respiration:
Place one hand behind the victim's neck. Tilt the head back with the other hand. This provides a clear, straight pathway from the mouth to the lungs.

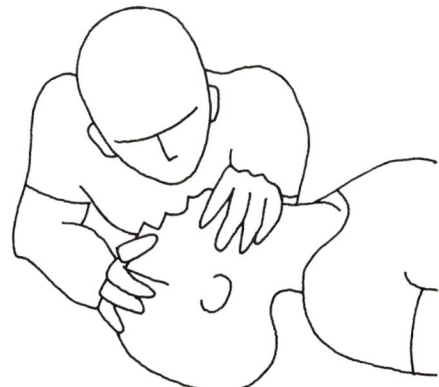

Support the neck with one hand and pinch the nostrils with the other hand.

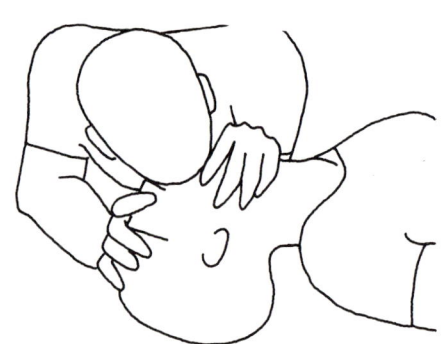  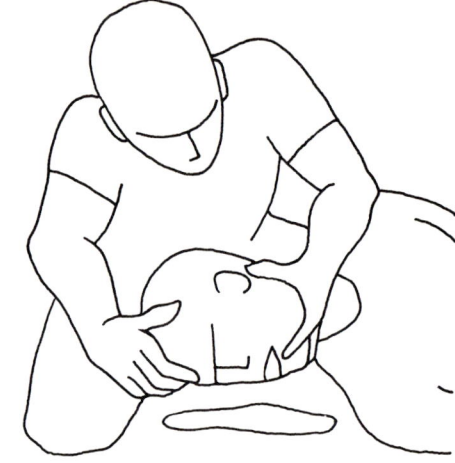

Take a deep breath and, sealing the victim's lips with your own, blow air into his mouth. The victim's chest should rise as air is forced into his lungs.

Remove your mouth and temporarily release the nostrils. The victim's chest should fall. Listen for escaping air.

If the air will not go in and the victim's chest fails to rise, check for blockages (e.g. vomit or swallowed tongue) in the air passage. Clear the passage and start again.

Repeat the first four steps rapidly several times before continuing to blow air into the victim's mouth at a normal breathing pace of about fifteen exhalations per minute. If the victim is a small child, increase the frequency of breathing and decrease the volume of air forced in. Check the chest cavity's rise and fall for verification of volume.

Approximately every five minutes, pause and check for spontaneous breathing on the part of the victim. If there is no sign of it, continue immediately with artificial respiration.

Cessation of Breathing For	Chances of Recovery
1 minute	98 saved out of 100
5 minutes	25 saved out of 100
10 minutes	1 saved out of 100
11 minutes	1 saved out of 1000
12 minutes	1 saved out of 100,000

Continue rescue breathing until the victim either recovers or is pronounced dead by a physician.

Mouth-to-mouth resuscitation should be commenced as soon as possible, whether in or out of the water. Chance for survival decreases rapidly, especially after seven minutes without respiration, so every second counts. As artificial respiration is continued, remove the victim from the water. Cover the victim with blankets, towels, or whatever happens to be available.

The skier should familiarize himself with other forms of artificial respiration which have been proven effective. These are the mouth-to-nose and the back pressure or Sylvester method. All skiers should be capable of removing a victim from the water, utilizing reaching assists, tending minor injuries, and approaching and towing a conscious or an unconscious victim.

Items which are useful to have around the ski dock are a spine board, a first aid kit, blankets, smelling salts, and possibly some inflatable splints.

SIGNALS

More specific to a waterskier's safety is the communication link between the boat and the skier. To ensure that both skier and driver know what is going to happen, a series of signals specific to waterskiing has been developed. They are as follows:

In gear... Hit it. When the skier is in the water ready to go up on his skis, he shouts "in gear" to the driver, who puts the engine in gear. As the boat moves away, the slack rope is drawn taut. The skier then yells "hit it" and the driver throttles forward, pulling the skier out of the water. Utilization of these commands provides for a safe start without any sudden jerks and without towropes tangling around the skier's arms or legs.

Okay signal. The skier clasps both hands over his head as soon as he recovers from a fall and he is sure he is not injured. He postpones looking for lost skis and immediately lets the observer know he is okay. The use of two arms is essential, as a one-arm wave could be misinterpreted as a wave for help, or it may be thought that the other arm is injured and cannot be raised.

Take me home. When the skier pats the top of his head, it means that he has had enough and he wishes to return to the starting point or to the dock area.

Okay signal

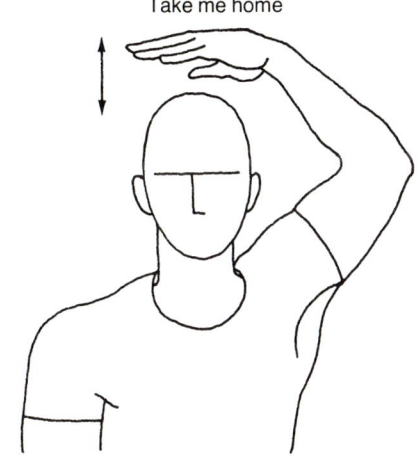
Take me home

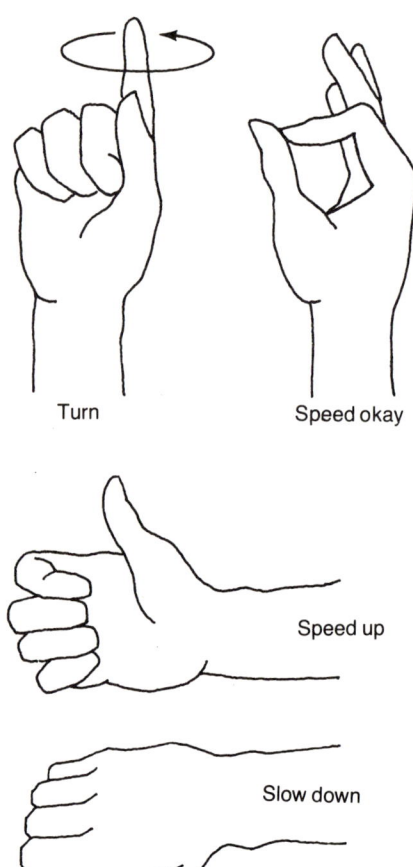

Turn. When either the skier or the driver uses a circling motion above his head with his arm, a need for a turn is indicated. Some people like to follow this gesture by pointing in the direction of the turn—this is optional.

Speed okay. An "O" made with the thumb and index finger is a sign that the skier is satisfied with the speed of the boat.

Speed up. The "thumbs up" gesture is used by the skier to indicate a desire for more speed.

Slow down. The "thumbs down" gesture is used by the skier to indicate that less speed is required.

Cut the engine. A "slit the throat" motion with the arm indicates that the boat is to be stopped immediately. This signal can be used by either driver, skier, or observer: the driver, when out of gas or trouble develops with the boat; the observer, to stop and give instruction; and the skier, to stop for a rest, fix some equipment, or request instruction. When this signal is given, the skier assumes a position directly behind the boat between the two wakes.

Skier in the water. The skier who falls and is left in an area of heavy traffic should tread water or float on his back with his head up and hold a ski vertically out of the water. This enables other boat drivers in the area to see him easily.

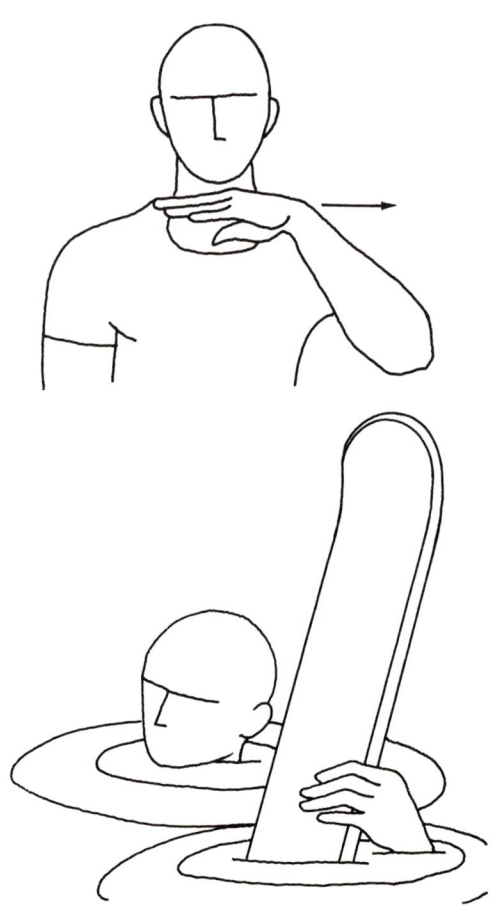

Both the driver and the observer should know these signals and use them.

Some skiers develop additional signals for even more effective communication between the skier and the boat. For instance, the observer may hold his arms extended to signal the skier that he should straighten his arms, or he may tap the underside of his chin to indicate that the skier should hold his head up. In any case, the signals listed above should be retained, as they are relatively universal in the waterskiing world and can be used virtually anywhere. If additional signals are developed, all those involved with the skier should be familiar with them.

EQUIPMENT

Skiers should be aware of the pieces of equipment which will help protect them from injury while skiing.

The most important piece of equipment is the jump jacket or the ski vest. Both of these will keep the skier afloat until a boat can recover him (although the skier's face may not stay out of the water if he is unconscious) and, because they are resilient, they will act as a cushion against impact with the water.

Good jump jackets and ski vests exhibit the following characteristics:
- The straps go completely around the body of the skier, either within the foam or outside the foam. Jackets with the straps on the outside are extremely useful for flat kite flying as they resist the tendency of the foam layers to split; the total pressure is exerted from the outside of the jacket. Straps are made of a nylon material.
- The color is relatively bright and contrasts with water color for easy spotting (e.g., red, yellow, orange).
- The foam is of the unicellular or ensolyte type and is covered with a vinyl water-repellent coating.
- A snug fit is essential. A skier should not buy a large jacket with the thought that he will grow into it. One jacket for two different sized persons will not do either. Loose jackets will slide up the body on impact and may slide right off, or the buckles may gash the skier's chest. The jacket must fit properly.
- Adjustable shoulder straps, though not essential, might prove an asset.
- The straps have to be long enough to go through the buckles, which should lock the straps in the position the skier desires.

Skiers are encouraged to use jackets or vests rather than belts. Belts tend to fall off or slide off during impact, they cannot float an unconscious skier, they fail to provide protection during impact, and generally they have a short life span. The value of a jacket is well worth the initial expense.

The wetsuit, which is closely related to the jump jacket, is currently popular with many skiers. Though not a safety feature in the same sense as the jump jacket, the wetsuit does afford some of the same cushioning effect during falls and does provide some flotation once the skier is in the water. It also provides warmth in cold waters. The wetsuit is used in addition to, not instead of, the jump jacket.

Several styles of wetsuits are available with a range of rubber thicknesses available in each style. When a skier purchases a wetsuit, he must check the suit for durability, comfort and usefulness.

- The best suits have seams which are glued with neoprene cement and then stitched. (Some have seams which are simply cross-stitched over elastic tape.)
- The best zippers are made of nylon because nylon requires a minimal amount of maintenance. Examine to see how the zipper is stitched into the suit.
- When being fitted for a suit, the skier should remember the principle of the wetsuit. Water occupies the space between the rubber suit and the wearer; this water is heated to body temperature, and it insulates the skier from the cold. Hence, the snugger the fit, the less water the body has to heat and the easier it is to retain that warmth.
- The suit should be comfortable, without a too-high collar or any other feature which might rub or chafe.

A helmet diminishes the risk of head injury during jumping. This is a relatively new piece of equipment and hopefully it will become a required part of the jumper's attire. As it is a new concept, no helmet specific to waterskiing has yet been developed. However, the light plastic suspension type with inflatable cells that is used for ice hockey is suitable. A second type which is acceptable is that used for snowmobile racing. It features a styrofoam interior and a nylon-cover capsule exterior. Both types are capable of floating and supporting the skier's head if necessary.

Observation of the safety guidelines established here and all safety regulations legally set forth in your skiing area will contribute to your skiing enjoyment. Use the signals. They are the skier's link with the boat driver. Your performance depends on his.

Chapter 2 Ski Boats and Driving

Anyone involved in waterskiing should take time not only to practice skiing, but should spend as many hours as possible driving the ski boat. A good skier understands the workings of boats and engines, knows how to operate and maintain them, and knows the nautical regulations of the area.

SKI BOATS

Almost any boat can be converted into a ski boat. For instance, although a 25 HP motor on an aluminum craft will not pull a 180-pound skier through a slalom course, it will be adequate in many instances for a youngster learning some basic tricks.

The ideal boat is the one which meets the skier's requirements. His choice of a boat is influenced by the size and number of skiers using the boat, the type of water conditions prevalent in his skiing area, the type of skiing in which he is most interested, whether the boat is to be used for recreation or for training and tournaments, the de-

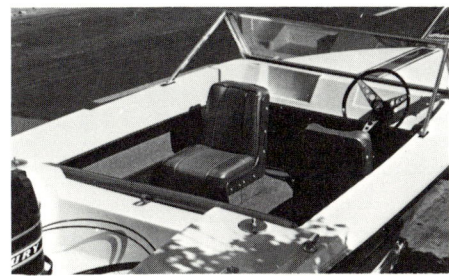

sired life span of the boat, and the amount of money the skier wishes to invest.

Many boats used by recreational skiers possess a deep or modified deep V-hull powered by an engine anywhere from 65 HP to 135 HP. Therefore, the recreational skier is usually equipped with a boat that is suitable for family boating as well as for recreational skiing.

Boats intended for such use should be comfortable with safe seating for all. A good unit to operate is a deep V-hulled boat with an engine which will ensure a speed of approximately 38 to 40 miles per hour while towing an adult skier. A boat capable of maintaining this speed enables the skier to partici-

pate in virtually all aspects of the sport, including kiting and barefooting. When purchasing a boat, it is a good idea to locate one in which the front passenger's seat can be rotated. This provides a comfortable chair for the observer. A consideration will be availability of space for locating a pylon. Some craft have seats which go right across the boat, making affixing of a tow bar virtually impossible. The throttle controls should be mounted in the center, so that both the driver and the observer can use the throttle effectively. The most significant reason for doing this involves safety in kite skiing. The advanced skier will undoubtedly wish to purchase a faster and more powerful boat. The type of ski boat chosen is determined by the skier's experience and the amount of money he wishes to spend. The powerful twin-engine boats are popular with advanced skiers. This type of boat, referred to as a *twin rig*, is frequently seen at ski tournaments held throughout the summer skiing season. Another feature of such ski boats is the hull design, which is a modification of the deep V-hull and displays a shallow, wide hull. There is some semblance of keel, adding to stability and maneuverability.

The inboard-outboard combines the power found in straight inboards with an increase in speed. These units are supplied with *power tilts*, which enable the driver to raise and lower the engine at will. By lowering the engine during takeoff, power is added to help pull up a skier, and by raising the engine after the boat has planed, velocity is increased (theory of engine tilt).

Unfortunately, many I/Os have unusually large wakes. This may be excellent for trick skiers, but it causes serious problems for slalom skiers and double-wake cut jumpers.

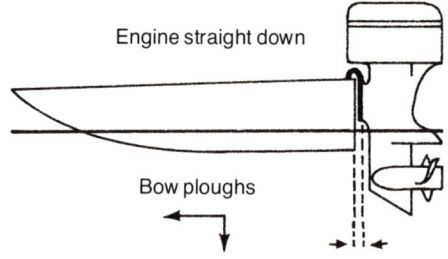

Engine straight down

Bow ploughs

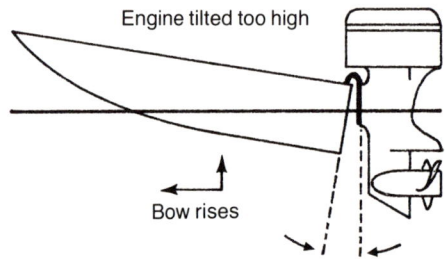

Engine tilted too high

Bow rises

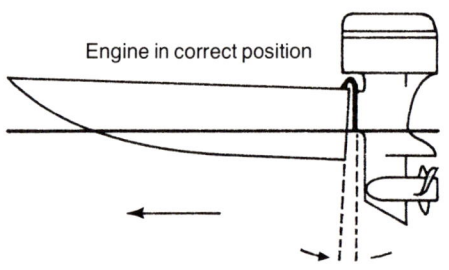

Engine in correct position

SKI BOAT EQUIPMENT

Following the purchase, the boat is ready to be fitted for use as a ski boat. The throttle control is placed on the left side of the driver in case the skier wishes to kite fly. The seat of the observer is reversed yielding him a comfortable view of the skier and providing a position from which he can throttle if necessary. A tachometer or speedometer which will not deviate in rough water is installed in the boat. Use of either of these is essential in all aspects of skiing.

Other equipment includes a fire extinguisher, a first-aid kit, two paddles, approved life jackets (one for each person in the boat and one for the skier), running lights, a sound horn, a bailing device, a ladder, two gas tanks, and mooring ropes.

Occasionally, ski boat operators like to include a mirror on their boat. A good type to install is a truck mirror, which is placed on the deck on its side.

Obviously the most important part of setting up a ski boat is attaching the rope. Several popular methods, from bridles at the back of the boat to bars over the engine, have been devised. The best device and quickest to work with is the *pylon* or *tripod* centrally installed in the boat. It is solidly affixed

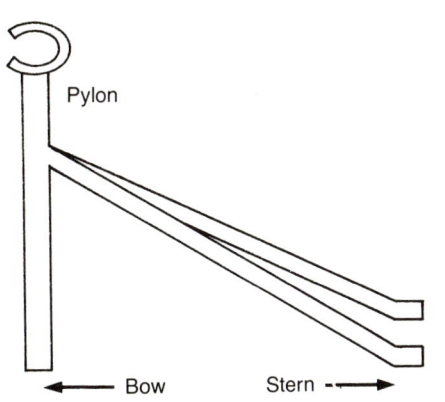

so that it won't pull out under extreme stress. Pylons which snap in and out with a minimum of effort are available. The appearance of the boat is retained as well as the space in the boat. A variety of top loops for the pylon are also available. The best of these can be used for all aspects of waterskiing.

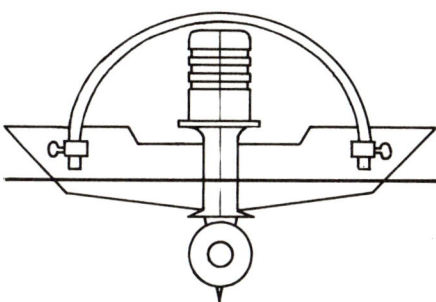

An extra bar made of metal or stiff plastic can be designed such that it goes over the motor and keeps the rope from catching on its various parts.

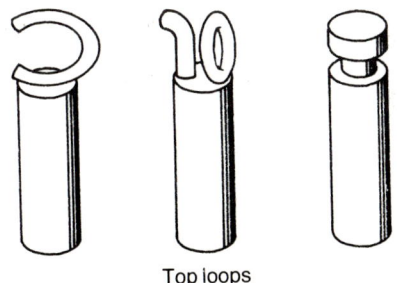

Top loops

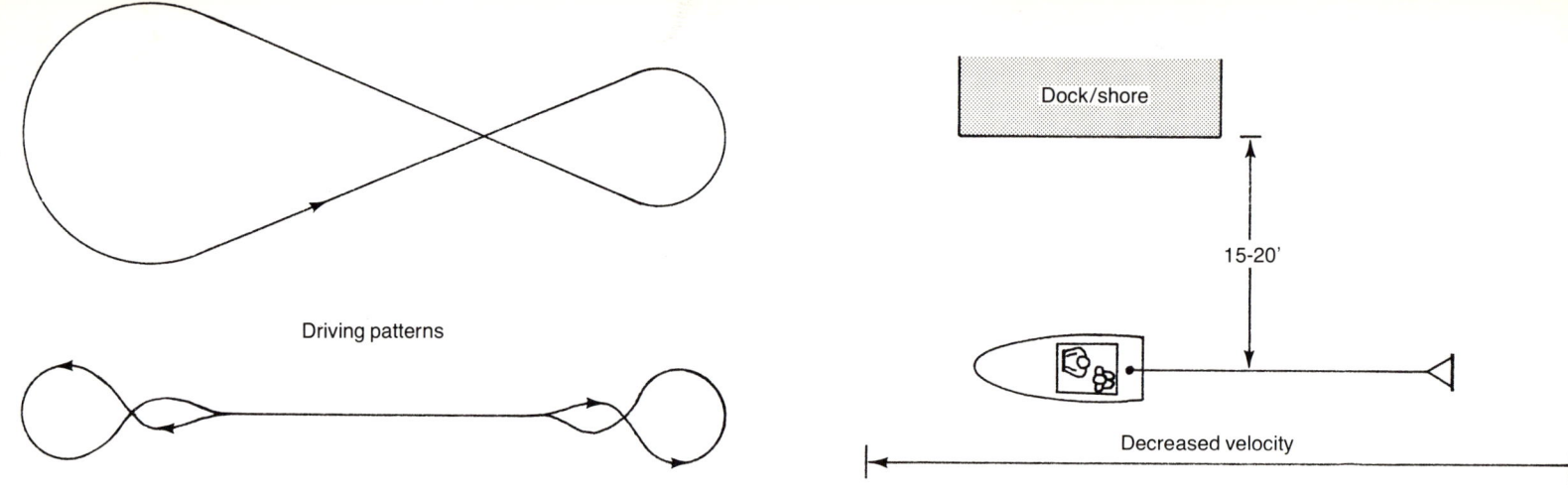

Driving patterns

DRIVING PATTERNS

With the appropriately equipped boat, the owner can start driving for water-skiers. Observance of local laws and safety regulations and the use of common sense will ensure a successful run.

Two patterns have been designed for skiers and should be used whenever possible. The best run for a skier minimizes boat wakes and turns and emphasizes straight runs. Therefore, straight lines as in the end loops pattern, are driven as much as possible. The figure-8 pattern is used in crowded areas.

Driving the same pattern all the time in the skiing area accustoms skiers and neighbourhood boaters to the driver's intent or habit and reduces the risk of accidents on the water.

The driver chooses a course according to the skier's ability and regulates and maintains speed appropriately. He lands the skier parallel to the dock or shoreline and far enough out that the skier will not injure himself on the dock or in shallow water. With beginner skiers, the driver slows the boat down when approaching the landing, allowing the skier to settle slowly and safely in the water.

PICKING UP A FALLEN SKIER

There are two methods for returning to a fallen skier. In both cases the driver must keep the skier on the driver's side of the boat and in view at all times.

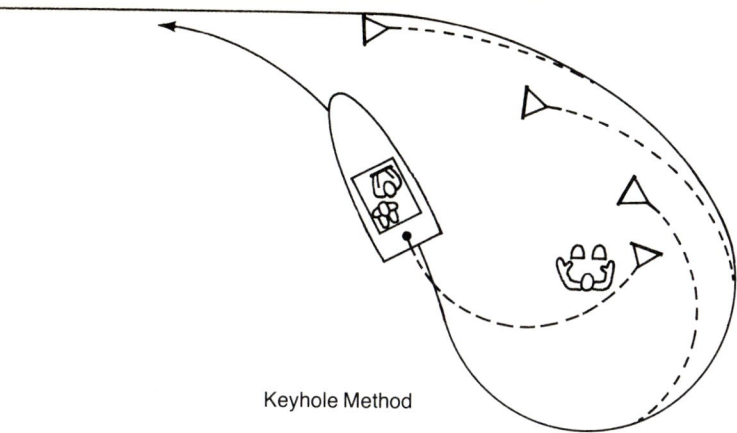

Keyhole Method

The Keyhole Method. The driver approaches with the skier on his side of the boat and circles him while maintaining a distance of at least 10 feet between boat and skier. The boat idles very slowly. Aid or instruction is easily issued from the boat at this distance. The driver maintains the slow speed all the while he is moving around the skier. He *idles out*, alternating from forward to neutral gear to prevent burning the skier's hands with the rope, and he is prepared to use reverse if necessary while the skier readies himself.

This is the best method for fallen skier pickup, both for giving instruction and for returning the rope to the skier. The rope comes right to the skier by his left shoulder. All he has to do is lift it over his head.

Half-turn Method

The Half-turn Method. This method of returning the rope to a fallen skier is especially useful with beginner skiers who might be confused by having to lift the rope over the head as in the keyhole method. Again, the skier is on the driver's side of the craft while the driver makes an idling approach. The boat approaches into the wind or into the current so that the boat is on the up side of the current and the rope floats to the skier, not away from him.

During pickups the observer plays a key role. He *immediately* informs the driver of a skier's fall. If the skier does not give the okay signal, the driver wastes no time in wheeling back to the injured skier. The boat approaches the skier at an idling speed and moves close enough for the observer to grab him.

In any pickup where the skier is near the boat for prolonged periods of time (i.e., receiving instruction or getting into the boat), the driver shuts off the engine.

All pickups of fallen skiers should display the same common sense and excellence of boat handling characteristic of all other facets of driving for skiers.

DRIVING FOR BEGINNERS

Driving for beginner skiers is a fine art and is just as difficult as tournament driving. It has been hypothesized that 85 per cent of getting a beginner up on water skis depends on the actions of the driver.

Deep-water starts

In starting the beginner, a relatively shallow area free of underwater hazards and swimmers is chosen. The skier stands there. He is lined up directly behind the boat. The observer looks forward for other boats. On the "in gear" command from either the skier or his instructor, the driver idles out into the water. He watchs the skier as he moves away. The rope draws taut, but does not drag the beginner (a slight touch of reverse is used if necessary).

When the "hit it" signal is given, a steady even forward throttle, sufficient to pull the skier out of the water, is applied. The boat moves forward in a straight line. An instructor in the water with the beginner, especially when the beginner is a young child, can use hand signals to avert a fear reaction or tenseup when the beginner hears "hit it".

Once the new skier is up, the speed is kept constant and adequate to keep him planing on the surface of the water. The driver turns in wide arcs, keeping the beginner behind the boat, and he allows wakes to dissipate somewhat before recrossing them. On landings, the driver slows the boat and skier down, keeping both parallel to the landing area.

Use of instructor signals from the boat increases the speed with which the beginner learns to ski.

Dock starts

Dock starts are similar to deep-water starts. The driver lines the skier behind the boat such that both are in a straight line when the boat idles out at a slow speed. On the signal from the skier, who is on the dock, the driver accelerates smoothly and quickly, pulling the skier off the dock. Once the skier is up, the driver looks forward and the observer looks back at the skier (a process known as overlap). Speed adjustment is achieved via communication between skier and observer, and then observer and driver. The driver should be ready to throttle when the skier has about ten feet of rope left, because the skier may ask him to hit it well before the rope draws taut. The driver, however, does not accelerate before the command is given.

DRIVING FOR SLALOM

Driving for slalom skiers is an advanced form of driving for beginner skiers. The driver must drive in straight lines (loop ends pattern), giving the skier a chance to perform his smooth rhythmic cuts. It is essential that the driver keep the speed constant. As skiers become more proficient, they cut harder. This exerts a pull on the boat. Failure of the driver to anticipate this pull causes slack rope, which throws the skier's timing off. A good slalom driver anticipates the pull of the skier and accelerates at this point to retain a constant velocity.

Maintaining a slalom speed of 20 to 36 miles per hour is no easy feat. It requires many hours of practice.

DRIVING FOR TRICK SKIING

The boat speed for trick skiing ranges between 13 and 20 miles per hour. The speed is critical. Good trick skiers can tell if the speed deviates by as little as one-half mile per hour when they're on the water. It is essential that the driver learns to use the speedometer or tachometer to its fullest. Anticipation is the key, with driver concentration at a maximum on skier wake turns.

In this case, communication between the driver and the skier is of supreme importance, and the proper use of signals is necessary.

Driver-observer communication is very critical when advanced trick skiers are behind the boat. Undoubtedly, the skier will be trying toehold tricks where he is bound to the boat with the normal rope, but his foot is held in a trap arrangement. In falls, the *bear trap* occasionally doesn't come off, and the skier is dragged by the boat. The observer must inform the driver of the fall immediately, and the driver must respond instantly by throttling down. This reduces the chance of injury to the skier.

It takes a great deal of patience on the part of the driver as well as skier and observer when someone is learning to trick ski. The driver should be prepared for hours of starting, stopping, and turning. He expects the same patience and courtesy when it is his turn to be the skier.

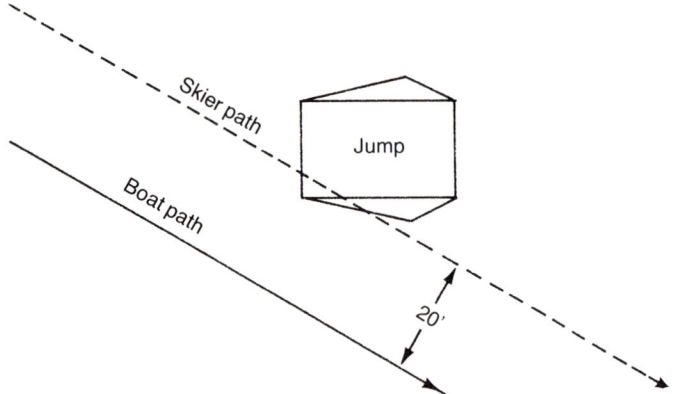

DRIVING FOR JUMPING

Driving for beginner jumpers differs from driving for advanced jumpers since speeds vary from 20 to 35 miles per hour.

The beginner is brought to the jump at a slight angle. Following the initial trips over the sides of the jump as the beginner gets the feel of the jump, the driver alters his course, bringing the skier in straight for his first trip over the top of the jump. The approach should be about 15 to 20 feet off the right corner of the ramp, and the driver concentrates on looking forward while the observer keeps him informed of the stages through which the novice jumper is passing. On these initial jumps, the driver *fans off* slightly as he passes the jump, thus taking up any slack which might develop in the rope.

If the skier wishes to continue, he is taken back through the same path in which he approached. Returning in this manner to reapproach reduces the amount of wake wash which will appear in successive approaches to the ramp and also in jump landings.

Some drivers use marker buoys off to the side of the jump combined with land markers either to the side of or in front of the boat to plan paths for the boat to follow. This is a good practice for any driver.

In advanced jumping, the same marker system can be implemented, but the buoys should be established at a distance from the right of the ramp (up to 38 feet). Again, they serve as a guide for drivers following the path.

Despite increased speeds of from 28 to 35 miles per hour found in this level of jumping, a hard cutting double-wake jumper will pull the boat back and occasionally pull it off course. As the driver experiences more advanced jumpers he will learn to adjust or anticipate and apply appropriate power as the cut commences. This is where an experienced observer is an asset.

DRIVING FOR KITE SKIING

Kite driving is a skill within a skill. It will be discussed later in the chapter dealing with kiting, and it is sufficient to say that the observer controls the throttle while the driver steers the boat in a straight line.

GENERAL POINTERS

A good driver takes the following into consideration:

- The driver is responsible for the safety of the skier, the observer, and the passengers. Before leaving the dock, the driver makes sure that the boat is gassed and that there are enough life jackets for everyone, including the skier. All safety equipment should be readily available. All passengers, including the observer, stay seated throughout the run. They may not move or stand up without the driver's permission. The driver and the skier are familiar with the course. There are no obstacles in the area which could cause injury.
- Many drivers are seen sitting either on the gunwales or on the back of the seat. The driver, the observer and the passengers should at all times be sitting in the seats.
- Nobody skis without an appropriate flotation device.
- Nobody skis after dark or before sunrise as the chance of an accident occurring is increased.
- The driver familiarizes himself with the boat he is asked to drive before he runs with a skier. Every boat has its own little idiosyncrasies such as variations in throttle tension adjustments and response, variations in the steering controls, or a finicky engine. The driver must be able to handle these.
- The driver takes care of the boat no matter who owns it. If it is his own, he waxes it with a good marine wax before the season. When the ski season starts, he gets up a half-hour earlier each day and scrubs the slime or algae from the bottom with a hard brush, washes and chamoises the top of the boat dry, and gasses up so the boat is ready to run. The driver sees that it is moored carefully. The boat bumpers should be adequate.
- The driver should know the skier's past experience and how he feels about the aspect of skiing he is about to tackle. The driver drives according to the skier's abilities. A fall could be detrimental to the skier's skiing future if he loses his confidence.
- The driver encourages the skier and gains his confidence through capable boat handling.
- Common sense and local regulations guide the driver in the formation of a skill as difficult to master as any in waterskiing. Good drivers are too few and far too important to be overlooked. Any skier will vouch that the excellence of the driver is directly reflected in the performance of the skier.
- Anyone wishing to become a driver should spend some hours as an observer and as a dockhand, working with and learning from the experienced drivers in the area.

Chapter 3   Beginner Two Ski

Skis

Water skis are selected with extreme care, and the type chosen depends on the age and size of the skier as well as the amount he wishes to spend. If children will be skiing and learning a great deal with an adult, it is beneficial for them to have their own skis.

Children's beginner or pairs skis are approximately 55 inches long and 6 inches wide. They are outfitted with bindings that fit a child's foot. The decreased ski size and foot size gives the child better control and affords him a better chance to succeed than larger skis would.

Adults' skis are much larger with an appropriate increase in foot or binding size. They are tailored to support a larger skier travelling at a faster speed. An adult can handle the increased size of the ski and he needs the extra support on the water.

Skis are now made of a variety of fibers and woods, and special attention must be given to the material when choosing skis. They must exhibit

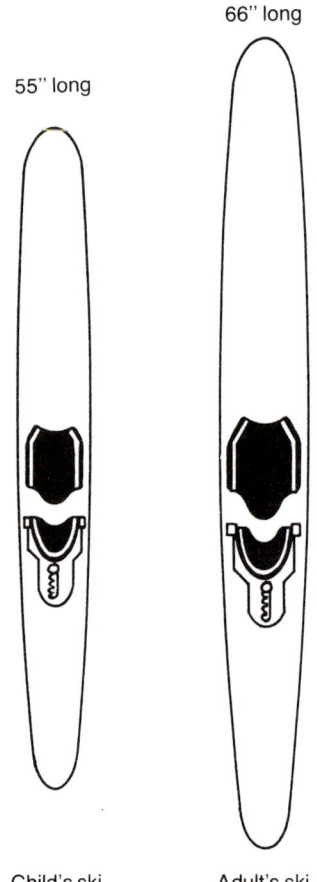

55" long

66" long

Child's ski   Adult's ski

strength and resilience, yet be stiff enough to permit control and stability on the water. The materials available include fiberglass, melamine, and wood. Melamine skis are not made exclusively of that material, but have a wooden core and a melamine top. Wood skis purchased should be of white ash. The grain of the skis and any laminations must be examined for defects or separations. No knots or bruises should appear in the wood. These could prove to be weak spots or sources of moisture in the skis.

Keels on the skis should be durable. On beginner pairs, which are liable to take severe punishment, the keel should not be made of narrow plastic or any material which is susceptible to breaking. Wooden or metal keels are the most durable under the circumstances.

When skis are purchased, the skier should be given a written warranty assuring him that damages in construction will be readily repaired or the skis will be replaced. Additional replacement parts should be readily available so that ski time will not be interrupted should the need for repair occur.

Bindings

The best bindings are made of pure gum rubber or molded rubber. These provide the best fit and most secure or snug grip. If properly taken care of, the gum rubber binding will last for many years. A second type of binding that has come into popularity recently is the formulastic binding produced in California. It is a rubber-type binder which provides all the comfort and security of rubber, but is free from most of the maintenance problems of rubber (e.g., rot due to sun rays or exposure to salt water). Though other types of bindings are available, gum rubber and formulastic have proven to be the best fitting and most durable.

Bindings are affixed to the skis with non-rusting metal components (e.g., aluminum, stainless steel). The bindings should be easy to adjust and there should be some type of locking mechanism to ensure that they won't slip while being used. There should be no parts which might have rough edges or sharp corners. These areas could cause injury to the skier. Skis with this type of binding indicate poor quality.

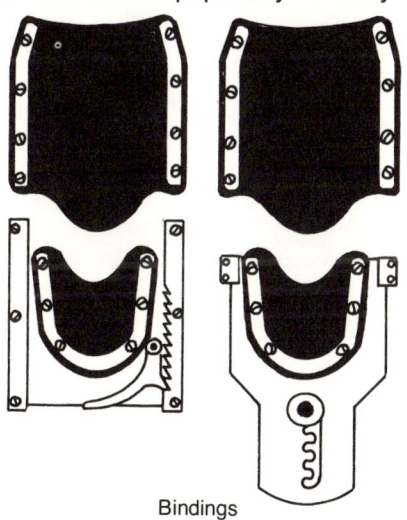

Bindings

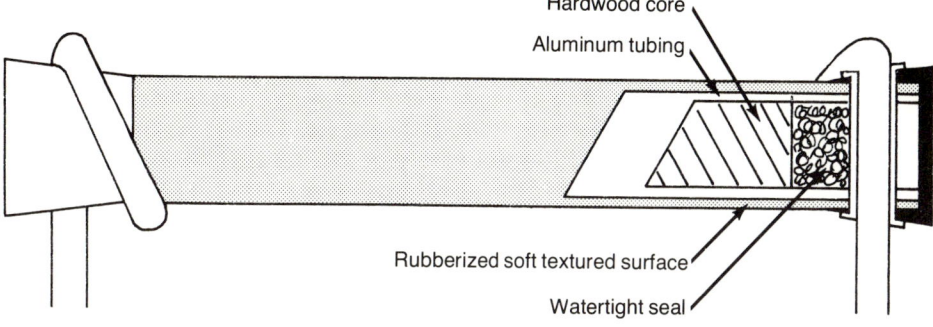

Rope and Handle

The towrope should be 1/4-inch polypropylene or polyethylene and a minimum of 1100-pound test line. The 12- or 16-strand braided rope should be 75 feet in length from loop to handle and have a hollow core area to permit splicing. The best handle is made of aluminum filled with either a hardwood or cork core water-sealed to prevent rot or waterlogging. The ends should be capped and the whole handle attached to the rope either with an eye splice or lock splice. The handles are generally covered with a foam coating which is soft, yet firm, and textured to provide a good gripping surface. The foam coating should be affixed to the handle and should not shift around it. Shifting will cause the rubber or foam to rip when placed under constant or extreme use.

27

DRY-LAND INSTRUCTION

Throughout this book dry-land instruction will precede doing the skill on the water. Every skier should attempt the new skill in a land simulated drill before doing it on the water. There is a sound physiological basis for this. If the skill/task is done correctly on land first, it stands a far greater chance of being successfully completed on the water. This procedure also enables the instructor to detect and correct major errors, saves gas and time, and enhances everyone's enjoyment of the sport. The dry-land exercises must be perfected before attempting the techniques on the water.

Getting Up on the Skis

With an assistant simulating the pull of the boat, assume a sitting position on the dock with knees pulled into the chest and heels pulled in close to the buttocks. With feet flat on the dock, extend the arms forward, one on either side of the knees. With tension on the rope, hold this position.

The assistant (the simulated boat) pulls the skier to the standing position. Knees are bent, elbows are straight and the head is up. These positions must be correct before proceeding. If not, repeat this step.

Next, wet both the feet and the ski bindings. This allows the skis to slide on easily. As the assistant holds the bindings, slip your feet into the skis. Make sure that the bindings are properly adjusted and that they fit snugly but comfortably. Do not worry about the bindings being too tight. In a fall, the skis will come off quite easily.

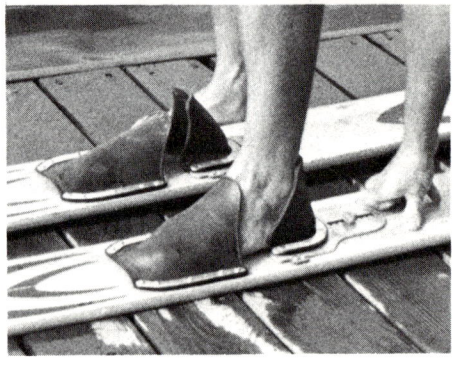

Assume the sitting position on the skis with knees bent up to the chest, heels in, arms forward with elbows straight and head up. Sit on the backs of the skis.

Again, the boat pull is simulated and the skier is pulled up. The skier does not pull himself up. The boat does the work.

The skier rises to the correct skiing position with knees bent, arms straight and head up. Body weight or the center of gravity is directly over the skis.

Practice this several times on the dock making sure that the boat does the work and that the skier ends up in the proper skiing position.

WATER PRACTICE

Deep-Water/Shallow-Water Start

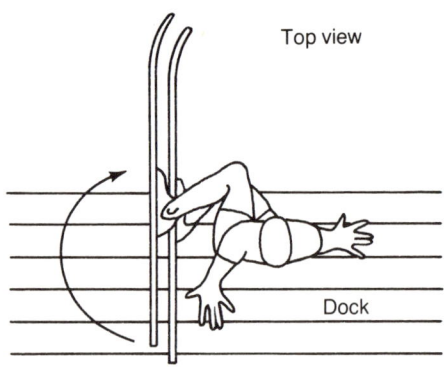

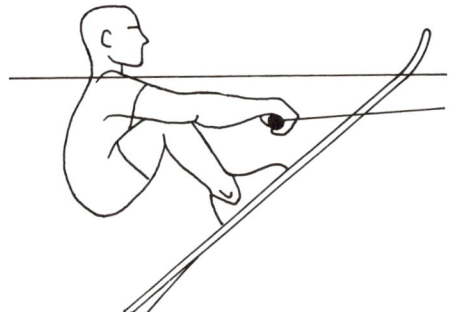

Move towards the edge of the dock and sit immediately to the right of the skis.
Swing both skis out to the left and into the water.

Slide into the water and move out several feet from the dock. (The ideal depth of the water is about 3 to 4 feet, but it may be deeper). Take the rope from an assistant on the dock. Carefully place the line between the skis. When the rope becomes taut, assume the beginner's position (knees bent up to the chest, arms straight on either side of the knees, and eyes looking at the boat).

When ready, give the driver the hit it signal and let the boat pull you out of the water as in dry-land practice.

When on the surface, the knees are bent, the arms are straight, and the eyes are looking ahead.

FALSE STARTS

Beginners who are having trouble getting up on the water should make only three attempts. Generally a beginner is tired after three attempts and further tries without a rest will only discourage him.

If the skier falls to the side, an uneven weight distribution where one leg is carrying the bulk of the weight may be the cause. He is leaning to one side too much.

If the skier is falling backwards, he is pulling in on the rope when he is getting up. The skier corrects this and is given a second chance.

If he is falling forward, he may be straightening his legs too soon, allowing the boat to pull him right over.

Repeated trys may prove fruitless in some cases. If this happens, numerous techniques can be implemented to get the skier up. An experienced person may assist the skier to hold his position in the water. If the start is in shallow water, the assistant simply stands behind the skier, holds him around the body and grasps him behind the knees. As the boat starts to move forward, both skier and assistant move forward with the assistant giving progressively less support to the beginner. In this instance, it is the assistant in the water who signals the boat driver to "hit it". He does this by nodding his head or by using some other prearranged signal. It is also a good idea in the case of young children for the assistant to talk to the child during the start. This reassures the beginner and instills confidence.

A second method of assisting starts is carried out in deep water off the end of the dock. In this case, the skier merely needs additional support while in the water waiting for the start. The assistant sits on the dock and hooks his feet under the beginner's arms or reaches down and places his arms under those of the beginner and supports him in the water. As the boat pulls away on his signal, the assistant gradually releases the beginner.

In extreme cases, an experienced instructor may be required to get into the water on skis and go up with the skier. Two different types of assists are available here, and both are characterized by the constant verbal assurances of the instructor. This relaxes the beginner while it reminds him of those points which will ensure his success.

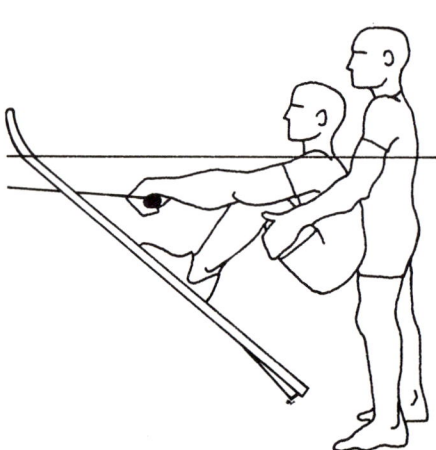

  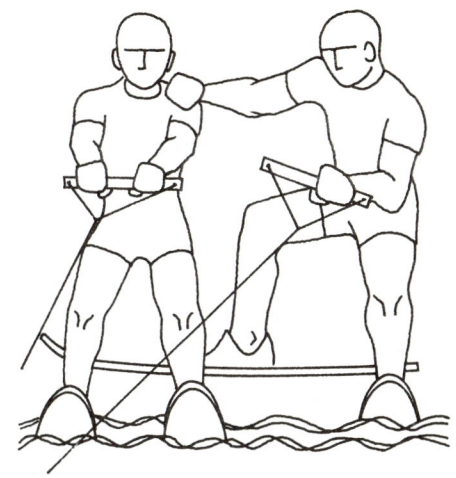

The Arm Lock Method.

Both the instructor and beginner have identical length ropes. When the beginner assumes his position in the water, the instructor holds either the near arm above the elbow or goes under the near arm and grasps the other arm above the elbow. This provides stability and confidence, which the novice skier may be lacking. The instructor gives the "hit it" command to the driver. Additional leverage is given in the interlock method.

The Body Lock Method

This method is used for extremely awkward skiers and is characterized by the instructor using a slightly longer rope. The beginner wears his own skis and holds his own rope. The instructor and the beginner line up directly with the boat and the beginner stands immediately in front of the instructor. The instructor reaches around the beginner's body and holds the towrope in both hands. His arms go under the beginner's and exert enough pressure on the body to provide support. Simultaneously, the instructor assumes a sitting position such that the beginner is resting his weight on the instructor's thighs. The beginner will probably be successful, even if it appears at first that the instructor is carrying him around the course. Once the beginner is up, the instructor releases one hand from his tow handle and steps around the beginner, lifting the foot on the same side as he released his hand. He makes sure not to touch the beginner, who is now skiing on his own. He continues to ski beside the novice and corrects style faults and instills confidence.

In extreme cases, one rope may be shared by the instructor and the beginner. The instructor will carry the novice around the run, giving him the sensation of skiing. The communication with the driver is from the instructor and is usually non-verbal as this tends to prevent tension in a beginning skier.

PUTTING SKIS ON IN THE WATER

What may seem only a minor problem for the experienced skier can be a major problem for the beginner. In the event of a fall, the skier attempts to get up again if he is not too tired. This usually requires putting on the skis in the water.

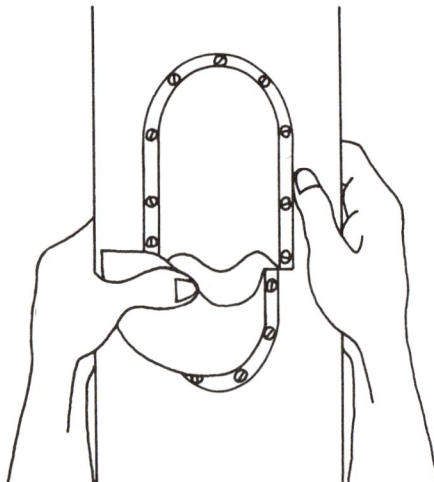

Grip the ski in the center near the binding. With the thumb, hold the heel piece to one side and jam the ski over the foot. The other leg is extended down in the water for stability. Once the foot is in the binding it generally stays there, and all that remains is to snap the heel piece up as practiced on shore. Placement of the second ski may be more difficult, but it can be put on in much the same manner. If difficulties arise, assume the snail position (jellyfish float). Duck your head under water, if necessary, and jam the toepiece over the toe in one swift movement.

If a loss of balance occurs during this process, it is imperative to remain calm and not struggle. Skis float, and so does the life jacket or vest. Just let everything float to the surface. Roll to the back position, if you are not already there, and stay there. Stability in the water can be attained by the arm action utilized in treading water or by a fanning motion.

Once the skis are on and the tips are up, assume the starting position.

CONTROL

Once the skier has fallen and gotten up once or twice he should be relatively accustomed to the skis. The next skill to master is turning.

Turning

Turns should be mastered inside the wake first. Beginners wishing to turn left put their weight on the left ski, and those turning right, on the right ski. The weighting on the appropriate ski is accompanied by a slight lean in the direction of the turn. This accelerates the cornering action.

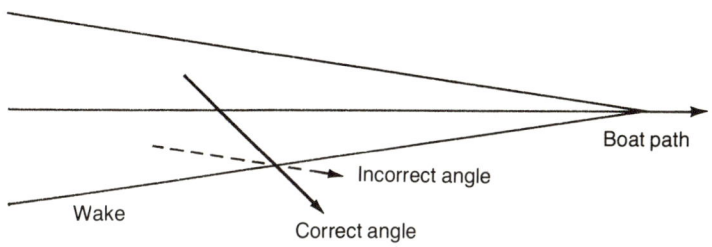
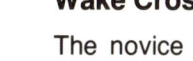

Wake Crossing

The novice must cross the wake as quickly as possible and at a sharp angle from the path of the boat. This will prevent his getting caught in the wash of the boat wake. Invariably, skiers learning to cross the wake try to go over the wake one ski at a time.

The result is a fall caused by the wake washing over the top of one of the skis and *sinking* it, throwing the skier off balance.

When crossing the wake, the skier bends his knees. This absorbs the shock of the crossing and is good form for the beginner in any case.

As the skier improves his technique he will find that accelerated cornering can be achieved by utilization of the edges of the skis. Digging in with the inside edges of the skis and leaning in the appropriate direction will increase the speed of the turn.

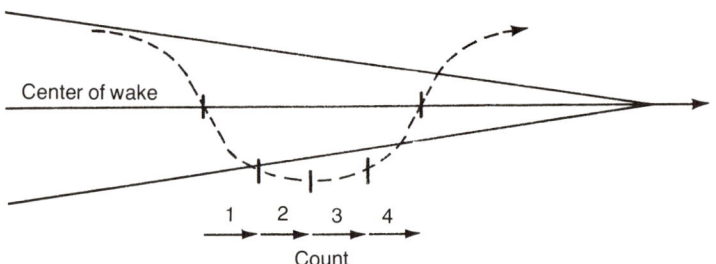

Rhythm

Much advanced skiing depends on one's rhythm. As technique improves, develop a rhythm of cutting. One method which generally proves successful is counting from the center of the wake to the outside of the corner and back. The count is the same for both sides (i.e., counts from center to center are even and generally cover the same area of skiing).

In developing a rhythm it is best to start with the cut just a few feet outside the wake on both sides and to gradually widen them.

Building a good rhythm sense enhances skiing at a later stage and makes each stage progressively easier.

Landing

Of course, there must be a way to get the skier down when he is tired. The boat driver gets the skier close enough to the dock or starting area, but it is up to the skier to drop off. He stays right behind the boat in between the wakes and as he approaches the landing area, he tosses the handle to the side away from shore. The best way for the skier to sink in the water is to sit on the water or fall backwards.

Two important points to remember when landing are a) to always land parallel to the shore or dock, never at right angles, and b) to land away from dangerous objects or areas. If approaching too fast, simply sit down in the water. This stops forward motion.

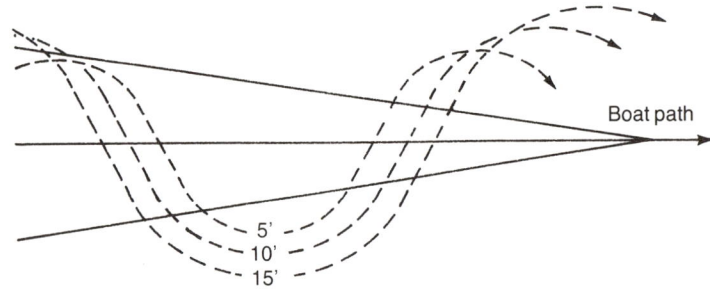

DOCK START (ADVANCED BEGINNER)

Once the deep-water start has been mastered and the skier is competent on the skis, he may try the dock start. The skier does not get wet, at the start of the run at least.

To accomplish this start, sit on the dock with the ski tips out of the water. In this start, as in the deep-water start, knees are bent to absorb shock. When the rope is about to go taut, lean the body slightly back and bend the arms slightly to absorb the initial pull of the boat.
Transfer your weight from the dock to the skis. The towline is held low, about waist high.

The position is very similar to the deep-water start in that the knees are bent, the arms are almost perfectly straight and the head is up with the eyes looking at the boat.
The boat *pulls* the skier off the dock. Keep relaxed and flexible while the boat does the work.

Chapter 4 Beginner One Ski

EQUIPMENT

Initially the beginner learns one ski by skiing on the same two skis utilized in learning two ski. After the skier accomplishes some preliminary maneuvers on the skis, he will need what is classified as a *slalom ski*.

The equipment for beginner one ski differs slightly from that used in two-ski skiing. The basic differences are in the binding placements, the shape of the ski, and the keel on the back of the ski. The keel, made of metal, is much deeper than a conventional pair skis keel. This enables the skier to have greater control of his maneuvering in the water. This ski responds more readily to changes in weight distribution. The bindings are similar to the adjustable ones found on the pairs ski. They may, however, be located further forward on the skis. A toepiece for the other foot is placed behind the front foot binder.

When selecting a slalom ski, examine the bindings and the material of which they are made. The materials

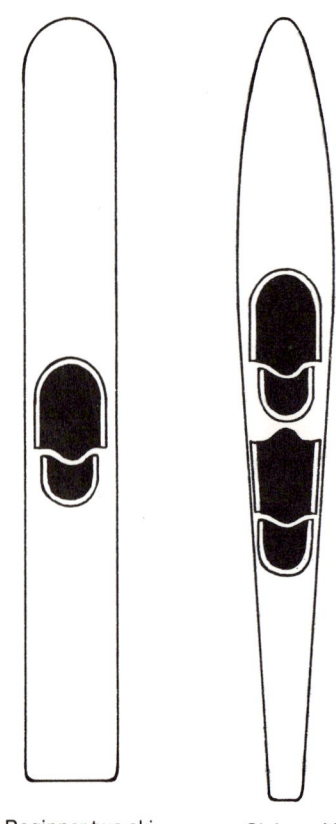

Beginner two ski   Slalom ski

suggested for two or pairs skis are the best selections here. A slalom ski is generally a more tapered ski than the pairs ski. The tip of the ski and the other end are narrower.

Some people who wish to learn how to ski and eventually how to slalom ski select skis which are referred to as *combo* or *combination pairs skis.* This is a pair of skis in which one ski is outfitted as a slalom ski. Initially, they appear to be an excellent value, but they rarely are. Combo skis attempt to combine the features of two distinctly different skis. Often there is no taper on the ski which is to be utilized as the single ski, and, more frequently, the keel, which is placed on the bottom, is a compromise between a pairs keel and a slalom keel in both depth and shape. A slalom ski often has the binding located nearer to the front of the ski. This feature is usually neglected on the combo skis. For these reasons it is a good idea to use extreme caution when purchasing combination pairs skis.

DRY-LAND PRACTICE

Skiing on One Leg

The dry-land technique should be used before attempting the procedure on the water. Establish the strongest leg and put the slalom ski on that foot. Loosen the other binding a little and place the wet foot into it.

With an assistant holding the rope, practice sliding the drop foot back, putting pressure on the toe and raising the heel out of the binding. Keep the weight slightly over the slalom leg. The water will sweep the ski away from the unweighted foot.
When the ski is being swept away, the toe comes right out of the ski and drags on the water. Point that toe backwards to help keep your balance. It acts somewhat like a rudder or auxiliary ski.

To counteract a loss of balance, put a slight bit of pressure on the free foot. A second reason for dragging the toe backwards is that the foot will be back by the toepiece when the skier wants to slip it in.
Practice the drag action on land after dropping the ski. If the action is done correctly on land, it should be easy to do on the water.

Keep the head up at all times and watch the boat. Do not look down at any time. Looking down is suggestive and usually results in a fall. Keep arms straight as in pairs skiing.

WATER PRACTICE

Establishing the strong leg

Using two or pairs skis, ski in the center of the wakes behind the boat and keep arms straight and head up.

Lift one ski and then the other. The one on which the skier feels most stable or the one which feels the stronger is the slalom leg. It will be the leg which is put forward on the slalom ski. Carry an extra ski in the boat; it will save time later.

Stepping Out

After discovering the balance leg, go behind the boat in the center of the wakes, and try again to lift the ski which you are going to drop. Do this several times.

Signal the observer when you are ready to lift the heel as practiced on land.

Do this gradually and let the water sweep the free ski away.

The water pressure pushes the free leg back, where it is left with the toe pointed downwards until balance has been well secured.

When you are well balanced (this may not happen on the first run or two), move the free foot over on to the back of the ski. Do not look down, but feel for the back of the ski. Once the foot is on the back end of the ski, it is a simple matter to edge it up and into the back toepiece.

Knees are slightly bent throughout this whole operation to accept much of the shock of small waves.

It is important that the whole movement, from dropping the ski to putting the free foot on to the back of the slalom, is done slowly and smoothly. Quick jerky movement throws the skier off balance and results in a fall.

TURNING

Turns are executed on one ski in much the same manner as on two skis. With the deeper keel and all the skier's weight on one ski, the ski responds much faster than two skis and the skier crosses the wake quickly.

When turning, lean the body in the direction of the turn and follow the ski around. Practice inside the wakes first.

THE BASEBALL GRIP

The baseball grip can be used for slalom skiing and jumping, but not for trick skiing. Grip the handle as if it were a baseball bat. Hands face in opposite directions.

CROSSING THE WAKE

Crossing the wake on one ski is achieved in much the same manner as on two skis—quickly and at right angles to the path of the boat. When crossing the wakes the first few times, skiers bend their knees much more than on two ski turns. This enables them to cushion the shock of the wake.

With the new skill and the new grip, work on a smooth, even crossing of the wakes. Take a rest after each set of six crosses. At first, the skier crosses about three feet outside the wake. Count out the rhythm and have the observer do the same. The count should be even on both sides with the

distance travelled approximately even as well. As the rhythm is perfected, gradually make the cuts wider from the wakes and retain the rhythm all the time. The turns should be smooth, rhythmic and continuous on all cuts.

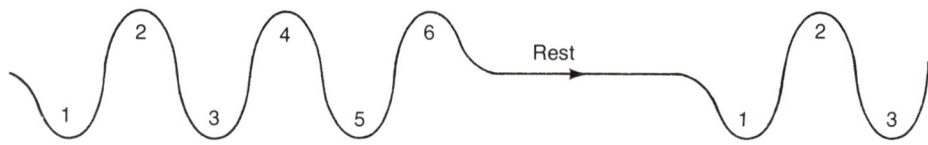

DEEP-WATER STARTS

It is inherent in waterskiing and learning new techniques such as slalom skiing that a skier will fall in the process. To slalom ski, it is necessary to learn to get up on one ski in deep water.

One-ski, deep-water starts are much the same as two-ski, deep-water starts. There are a few tricks which are an asset in getting up on one ski.

Place the rope on the instep side of the ski. The ski rope will be on the free leg side of the ski.

When the rope draws taut, bring the ski leg up until the knee touches the chest as in starting out on two skis.

The free leg is then extended straight back where it acts as a rudder or auxiliary ski and stabilizes the skier.

Point the toe back. Bend the arms slightly and keep body weight evenly distributed over the ski.

The position with the leg extended back, toe pointed, arms slightly bent, weight over the ski and head up is maintained until a balanced position on the water is attained. The back foot is not put in the binding until the skier is well balanced.

The key to the whole sequence is keeping the back leg perfectly straight. It provides stability and a buoyant force which lifts the skier up out of the water.

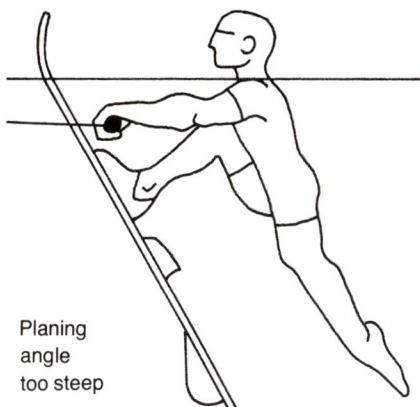

Planing angle too steep

If the skier has a great deal of trouble pulling out of the water; that is, if he is being pulled for long distances in the water until he tires or gives up, the plane of the ski in the water may need to be adjusted. The ski may be tipping up such that a wall of water is pushed in front of the skier. In this case, the ski

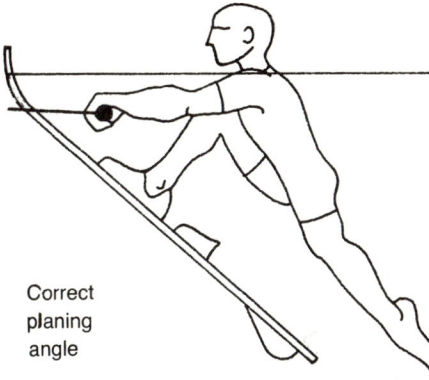

Correct planing angle

is flattened out on the surface of the water a little. This allows the ski to plane out more quickly and support the skier on the surface. The altering of the plane or angle of the ski in the water is not accomplished by moving the knee away from the body. It is achieved by flexing the knee more and contracting the ankle.

DOCK STARTS

Some skiers who work with just one ski don't want to get wet right away. Two methods have been devised for getting them on to the water.

Sitting Dock Start

This is basically the same as the two-ski dock start.
Sit on the edge of the dock as the boat slowly idles straight out from the dock. Depending on the power and speed of planing of the boat adjust the amount of slack taken in the rope. Generally, about two coils of rope (8 to 10 feet) are taken for slack.
On the appropriate signal, the driver accelerates while the skier leans back slightly on the dock with knees and arms bent and head up. The boat pulls him off the dock just as in the two-ski dock start.
The leg is dragged back for support until the skier is balanced, at which time the toe is tucked in the binding.

Jumping Dock Start

Some skiers go for a little more style in the dock starts and prefer the jump start to the sitting dock start. The basics are the same in both cases: the slack rope, the bent arms and knees, and the correctly timed lean back. This time, however, the effort must be co-ordinated with a correctly timed hop off the dock.

Stand on the dock with your foot in the slalom ski.
The ski's keel must be free of any cracks or obstructions on the dock.
The slalom toepiece is placed at the edge of the dock.

Take about 10 feet of rope (depending on the boat and motor) as slack and put your weight on the free foot on the dock.

A skier who is learning the jump start from the dock might find it easier to insert intermediate steps. This is an excellent idea if the skier is working from a high dock. He places the ski off the edge of the dock and transfers his weight to the ski as the rope tightens. Each consecutive step takes the previous one a little further, and the cycle described above is completed. Skiers who have trouble with the first style can utilize this method of breaking down the steps.

As the boat accelerates away from the dock, time the leap from the dock so that the ski will hit the water either just before or just as the rope draws taut.
The jump is led by the ski, and the body weight is kept slightly back and over the ski. It is initiated from the free foot.

LANDING

When a skier perfects one ski he tends to hot-dog it a little. Land parallel to the dock or shore line, never at right angles. Never take a run where you could end up coming in too close and have to swerve at the last moment. During that swerve the keel could skip out of the water and send you flying into the air and crashing into the dock. When landing, try not to create a wall of spray right at the dock. No spectator wants to get wet by a shower of spray from some waterskier who is showing off his newly acquired skills.

The legs are bent as are the arms, and the head is kept up. The free leg is back and the toe pointed until balance is attained.

Chapter 5 Slalom Skiing

SKIS

More work has gone into the design and construction of the slalom ski than any other piece of waterskiing equipment.

Bottom

A large portion of this emphasis has been placed on the bottom surface of the ski. Initially a flat surface with squared edges, the slalom ski next featured an edge to edge concave surface with somewhat rounded edges. Since then numerous other modifications have taken place including grooves of varied configurations and the deep tunnel concave with the rounded or beveled edges. Each of the following designs has its distinctive advantages and performance traits.

Square edges. The flat bottom with square edges was the initial slalom ski design. It is a good learning ski for the beginner slalom skier.

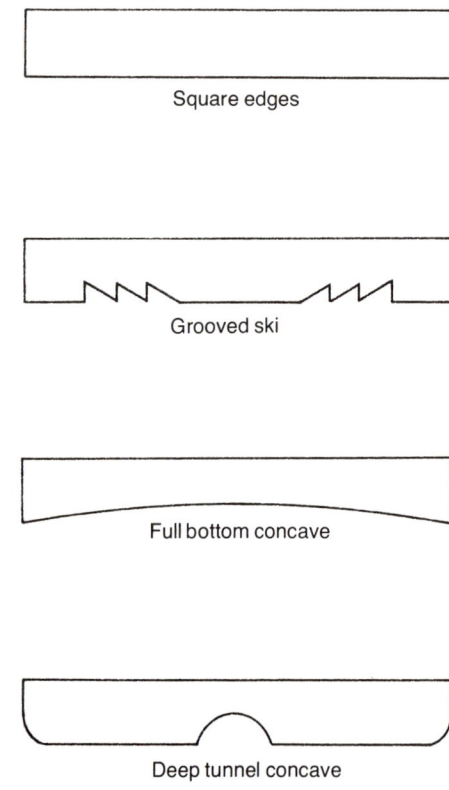

Square edges

Grooved ski

Full bottom concave

Deep tunnel concave

Grooved ski. Combined with the tapering of both toe and tail of the ski, the groove provided the next advancement for the water skier. It claimed to increase the cornering ability of the ski by holding it in the water, especially in calm water. Marketing made this ski a very popular model; however, it failed to live up to expectation in its performance.

Full bottom concave. This was the next advancement in the slalom line. It however had a tendency to wobble in the water. One had to ski on one edge or the other to get it to perform correctly. It did prove useful, however, for the light skier.

Deep tunnel concave. Progress provided the deep tunnel concave, a 1-1/2-inch wide by 1/2-inch deep trough down the center of the ski. However, the part of the ski which had no tunnel had a tendency to slip out of the water.

Deep tunnel concave with beveled edge

45° bevel

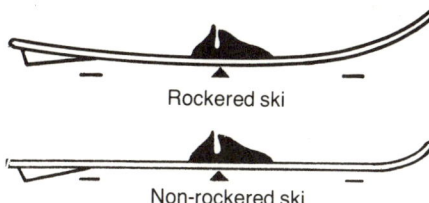

Rockered ski

Non-rockered ski

Deep tunnel concave with a beveled edge. The compromise slalom ski came with this design—a deep tunnel with a rounded beveled edge. This provided a dihedral effect (the ski is sucked down into the water). This design was the basis for such skis as the O'Brien, one of the first, the Maherajah, and numerous others.

Bevels

When purchasing a slalom ski, the differences in side bevel should be considered, as well as the advantages of one ski bottom over another. The bevel influences tracking (skiing in a straight line) when it is located at the back and cornering when it is at the center or the front portion of the ski. The bevel is the key to the dihedral effect of the ski.

Many of the newer, more advanced skis on the market have bevels as diagrammed. The better slaloms have altered the bevel along the ski, from tip to heel, to accommodate for those differences in cornering and tracking. The most advanced skis allow the skier to make his own alterations in bevel design, thus customizing the ski.

Rocker

The rocker is the *natural curvature* in the ski along the longitudinal axis. Rocker in a slalom ski influences the turning and the accelerating capacities of the ski.

The cumulative effect of bevel, rocker, and tunnel concave is to allow the ski to slide sideways in the water, while maintaining the dihedral effect around the corner.

Construction

Nearly all skis, slalom included, have been made of wood in the past. The trend now is to convert to some form of fiberglass epoxy ski. The numerous fiberglass skis that appear on the market today are constructed in different ways. Specifically, they differ in core design, and any reliable dealer will be glad to explain these differences to a skier. Regardless of the core design, the fiberglass ski offers several advantages over the wooden ski.

The *glass* slalom ski can be engineered and molded to provide the desired amount of flex or stiffness at any location along the length of the ski. For instance, it is possible to make a ski which will react well when in rough water or when crossing the wake by making the tip extra stiff and allowing more flex in the tail for acceleration and cornering purposes.

As well as maximizing control of flexural patterns in the ski, a computer designed ski can produce significant improvements in rocker and bevel design. Further, fiberglass slalom skis afford the skier lightness in weight and ease of maintenance.

As with fiberglass trick skis and jumpers, slalom skis retain their shape, remaining unaffected by changes in climate or by time. This is advantageous for the northern waterskier, who is forced to store his equipment in the off-season. The ski will appear the following season in the same condition as it did in the previous season.

Obviously, the high speed fiberglass slalom skis have numerous advantages over the average wooden ski. This is not to say that all wooden skis are inferior. On the contrary, many offer excellent value.

Some wooden slaloms, which have seventeen or more laminations in various configurations, are strong and durable skis (e.g., Maherajah, O'Brien). The flexural pattern and shape retention can be controlled to a degree by the laminations involved.

Repairing and customizing these skis are both matters of relative ease. With their attractive grain finishes and their proven performance, these skis can provide hours of enjoyment and success for any slalomer.

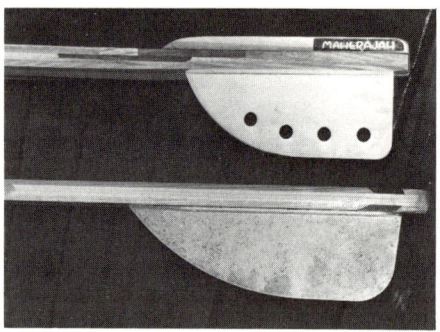

Keel

High speed slaloms have a specific type of keel. The keel, made of aluminum, is usually of the drop through design, which gives added stability to the fin. Unlike the beginner slalom ski keel, the high speed slalom keel has holes in it. These holes eliminate the possibility of a pressure area or air pocket forming under the keel and "popping" the ski out of the water. In calm waters, the holes add to the cornering abilities of the ski by holding it in the water. The number of holes in the keel is a matter of personal preference.

Bindings

A high speed slalom ski requires special bindings. The bindings in the competition or high speed slalom have fixed heel pieces. Because they are unadjustable, they ensure an extremely tight fit and a highly personalized ski. The high toepiece and heel piece give maximum support to the skier's front foot and ankle and ensure a perpendicular angle between the ski and the skier's leg. The bindings on the high speed ski are generally placed forward with the center of gravity over the fulcrum point of the ski.

The toepiece for the rear foot is located in close proximity to the front binding. The high heel piece in the rear binding guarantees the slalom skier stability and maintenance of rear leg position on the water ski. Different manufacturers' bindings vary, and it is up to the skier to select those which afford him a snug fit as well as comfort and durability.

Purchase of an advanced or high speed slalom is a major decision and one to be thoroughly considered before making an investment of this magnitude. Selection of the ski is dependent upon the ability, height and weight of the skier and the speed at which he skis, as well as upon his personal preferences. With changes occurring in design and construction of skis as rapidly as they are, it is best to discuss the selection of skis with a reputable dealer and to try out a sample of the ski for a few runs if possible.

OTHER EQUIPMENT

In addition to a good ski, a good rope is a necessity for the slalom skier. It should be made of diamond-braided polypropylene and be 75 feet 4 inches long with shortening loops (necessary for competition) at 15 feet 6 inches, 22 feet 10 inches, 28 feet, 32 feet, 36 feet, and 38 feet 8 inches. The handle should be of the type previously recommended.

The jump jacket is essential in case of high impact falls which sometimes occur in slalom.

Gloves and a ski bag are also good ideas for the slalom skier.

FREE SLALOM SKIING

Prior to running through the slalom course, the skier should spend time accommodating himself to the ski. The ski virtually becomes a part of him. Practice cutting and wake jumping, skiing with the weight distributed over various parts of the ski (e.g., with the weight forward, then as far back as possible) to see and feel exactly how the ski responds. Test the edges on both sides of the ski to learn how they function.

Much can be done outside the slalom course to develop style. Count out the rhythm. The observer can see if the cuts are late or farther out on one side than the other. Make the turns in smooth, rhythmic arcs and in sets of six with a short rest between each set. The turning sequence outside the course is the same as in the course; hence, they can be practiced while free skiing.

Ski to approximately 35 to 40 feet outside of the wake.

Slow down upon approaching the focal point of the corner by transferring the weight to the front foot and bending forward slightly.

Rounding the corner, bring the outside hand back to the handle. Pull the rope against the boat and low to the hip area.

Pull hard until you cross the second wake.

Extend the inside arm straight out towards the boat and drop the outside arm from the handle.
Initiate the turn with an inward and downward pull of the rope to the hip. The weight is drawn back towards the rear of the ski as the skier rounds the corner. Hips, shoulders and head should be in a straight line throughout this weight transfer.

After running these patterns several times, the skier realizes that advanced slalom skiing is a series of transitional phases through which the skier must go during his run. It can be considered analogous to the action of a pendulum with its phases of acceleration and deceleration as the pendulum swings. The boat acts as the focal point of the pendulum, and the skier's turns follow the swinging pattern.

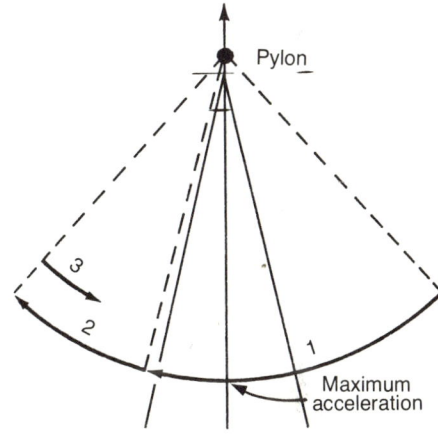

On the opposite side of the wake, repeat the sequence. Slow down or brake when approaching the corner by putting more ski into the water or transferring the weight over the front of the ski.

The pylon serves as the fulcrum or focal point of the pendulum. 1. Skier acceleration commences at the corner and continues to the second wake crossing. 2. Gravity causes deceleration from the second wake to the corner. 3. The transition zone for the skier is the area where he is between deceleration and acceleration. In the pendulum action, it is where the swing stops and acceleration in the opposite direction is about to begin.

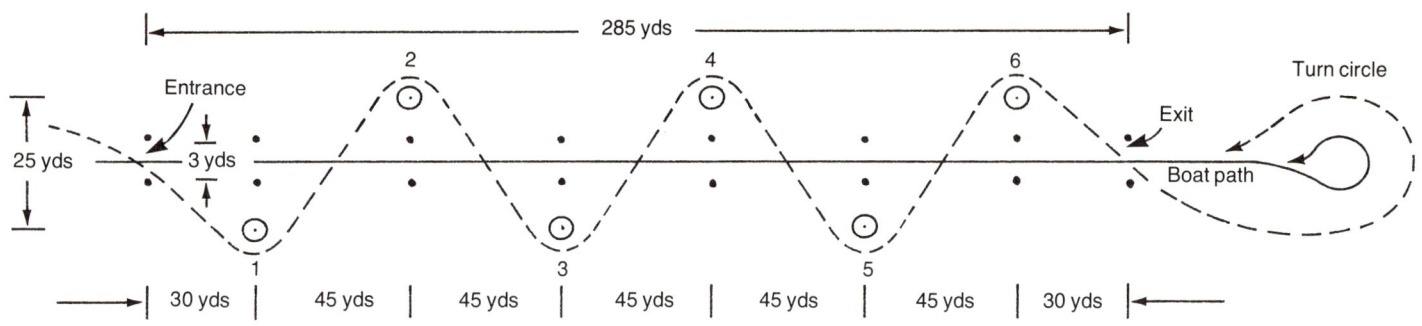

Slack Rope

Some slalom skiers frequently encounter a phenomena known as *slack line,* which occurs in rounding a buoy or corner. There are two major causes of slack line, the first one being a hook turn. This is when the skier (forgetting his smooth rhythmic arc) turns too sharply in towards the boat. The result is a slight pause following the turn while the boat takes up the slack. The skier is in a poor position at the next ball because of the deceleration instead of acceleration from the point of the turn. There is no problem if the smooth arc around the buoy is maintained with full extension of the body followed by full contraction.

A second major cause of slack is the skier continuing his pull beyond the second wake. His acceleration continues and the deceleration phase is cut short. Hence, when he turns toward the boat in his corner, he is travelling faster than the boat and with extra rope. This can be cured by returning to the sequence already established; that is, by dropping the outside arm and moving forward on the ski after the second wake.

A good rhythm and form while free skiing will definitely benefit the skier in his runs through a slalom course.

SLALOM COURSE

There are 6 slalom balls and 16 boat gates in a slalom course. (In tournament situations there are usually several judges' towers in close proximity to the course.) The skier running the slalom course must enter through the end two gates and run around the remainder of the balls as numbered before exiting between the balls at the opposite end of the course. He then turns and runs through the course again starting at this end.

A slalom course can be constructed in several ways, each ensuring accuracy in measurements and distances. Plans for such a construction as well as official rules for national and international slalom competition are available from the governing water ski body in your area or from a national skiing association.

RUNNING A SLALOM COURSE

A skier with developed ability may run the slalom course. The course indicates when the skier must make his turns and it provides a means of determining, in fair competition, who can manipulate the turns most efficiently.
Running a slalom course is no easy feat. It requires practice, ability, excellent physical condition, and continuous concentration.

Boat Pattern

On entering the slalom course, the speed of the boat should be between 24 and 36 miles per hour. Once in the course, the speed must remain constant throughout. The boat is driven in a straight line between the marker buoys, favoring neither one side nor the other.
The driver must learn to anticipate the pull of the slalom skier at each ball and complement with additional applied power such that the boat speed is constant and unwavering.

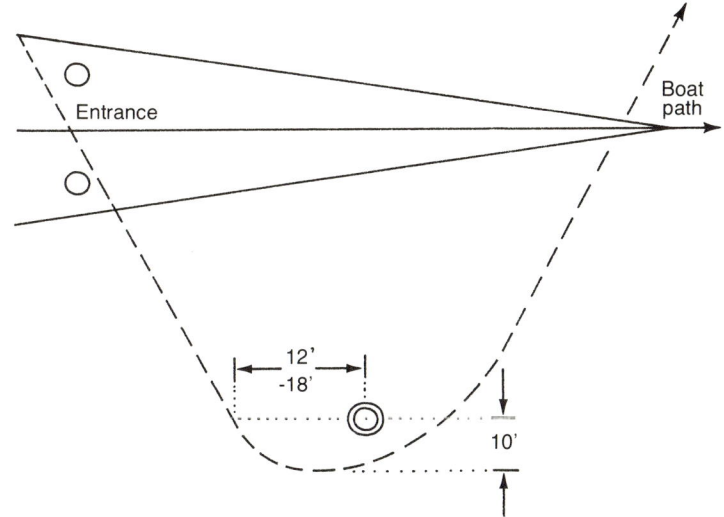

Skier Pattern

A correct entrance to a slalom run is the key to success throughout. If a skier can get a headstart at the first buoy, he should be well in advance for the rest of the run. To get this headstart, swing wide out to the left and cross both wakes to the right as you enter the course between the entrance gates.
The approach to the first ball should be in line with the entrance through the gate. As you cross the second wake, begin to decelerate, release the outside arm from the handle and extend the inside arm towards the boat as the weight is transferred forward on the ski. It is the same process which is used when free slalom skiing, only this time the turn is co-ordinated with the location of the balls.
At a point roughly 12 to 18 feet in front of the first ball and ten feet above it, transfer the weight back and pull against the boat as you draw the rope in low to the hip. This initiates the turn around the first ball.

53

As the turn is completed and you accelerate towards the second ball, you will pass the first ball on the downcourse side. You have actually completed the turn before the first ball and now have an excellent headstart on the second ball.

As in free slalom skiing, when crossing the second wake, release the outside hand from the handle and extend the inner arm out. Move the weight forward on the ski, pushing more of the ski into the water and causing a deceleration. A combination of body lean forward and maximal arm extension leaves you in a good position to take up slack, if there is any.

The turn on the second and subsequent balls should be initiated well in advance of the buoy, approximately 10 feet back and 10 feet above the ball. As in free skiing, it is initiated by the simultaneous weight transfer from front to back (leaning backwards with the hips, shoulders, knees and head in line) and a pull on the rope with both arms low and into the hip. The ski edge is firmly in the water and acceleration is rapid. Again the turn is completed and the skier accelerates towards the next ball as he passes the second one on the downcourse side.

Keep the weight back and concentrated against the pull of the boat. The rope should be low and in close to the hip. This lowers a skier's center of gravity, making him more stable and powerful, and it prevents him from breaking forward at the waist during the acceleration phase. At this stage, ride on the outside edge of the ski (i.e., going from the left side to the right side of the course, it would be the right edge).

Hold the pull across the second wake and repeat the whole process. Attempt each time to get outside the course. Try to complete the turn as you pass the next slalom ball.

When a skier becomes proficient, he will run through the slalom course with a shorter rope length. A ski club or a good instructor can coach a skier and improve his slalom style through the course.

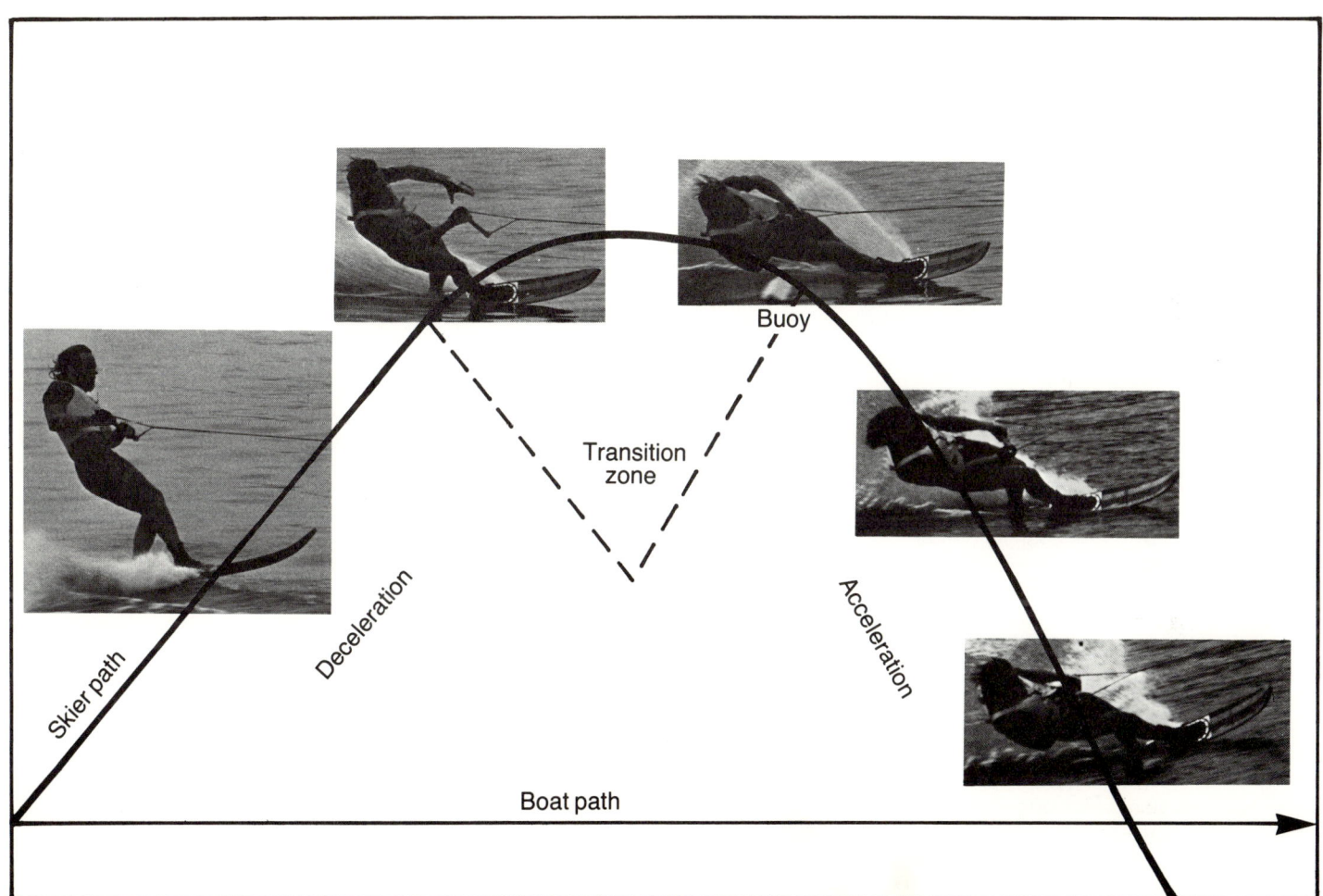

Chapter 6 Jumping

Jumping is perhaps the most exciting part of waterskiing, both for spectators and participants. Few other sports can equate the sensation a jumper feels as he leaves a ramp at 60 mph.

EQUIPMENT

Obviously the key piece of equipment for the jumper is the jump. A well-designed and well-constructed jump not only adds to the skier's performance, but is essential for his safety. Plans for a jump are available from either a national or a local ski organization.

Every jump should have side curtains to ensure skier safety. The double-wake jumper will be deflected from the underside of the jump should his cut be late.

The surface of the jump is also important. It should measure 14 feet by 25 feet and be free of any protruding objects such as nails. Not only can protrusions impair performance and present safety hazards, but they may damage expensive equipment by ripping gouges in the bottom of jumpers.

The ramp surface can be covered in several ways. The most conventional is to coat the jump with wax, usually 180°F melting point paraffin wax. Before the skier jumps, however, the surface must be wet either by hand or by using a water pump affixed to the jump. A second method of coating the surface of the jump is to use a synthetic material such as fiberglass-coated plywood sheets, Pandura, or special paints (e.g. Kem Glaze II). These generally require less work in terms of maintenance. Waxing may have to be done several times per season.

The jump should be built so that the height is from 3 feet to 6 feet (in competition men jump at 6 feet and women at 5 feet). This then affords an excellent competition jump as well as a good jump for teaching the beginner.

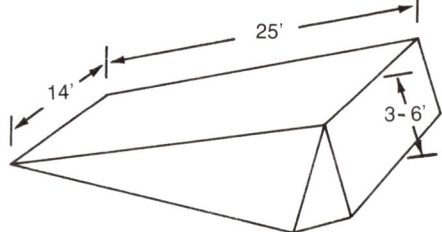

The ideal jump is adjustable from 3 feet to 6 feet, measures 25 feet by 14 feet, is well prepared on the surface with a substance such as wax, and is watered well.

The next most important step in equipping the jumper is providing safety equipment. Every jumper must wear a flotation device of the jump jacket type.

This also affords protection in high impact falls. Many jumpers wear wetsuits for added protection. An essential piece of the jumper's attire is a helmet. Every jumper should wear a helmet of a solid one-piece shell. Good hockey helmets have been adapted for this purpose.

Jump skis differ from conventional pairs skis in several ways. They can be made of wood or a fiberglass-composite structure. They are generally rockered and have bindings which provide support. On wooden skis the bindings are often mounted on a metal plate to dispurse impact and then mounted on the ski. If the ski breaks, the foot is well protected. The best bindings are pure gum rubber cut from a sheet, although molded rubber is popular as well.

Jump skis are subjected to tremendous amounts of pressure, both on the ramp and on landings. The traditional heavy reinforced wooden jumpers with metal tip plates have been replaced by relatively normal weight skis. Wood skis, while capable of withstanding many years of use, are generally not guaranteed because of the nature of the event and the extreme stresses placed on them.

Recently, jump skis, as with trick and slalom, are being constructed of fiberglass with varied core designs. Fiberglass jump skis offer advantages including a) lightness resulting in increased velocity on the water and decreased *drag* on the skier once airborne (a large portion of this may be psychological) and b) strength which often gives the skier more years of use and gives him an opportunity to accommodate himself to his skis. Any good fiberglass jumpers should bear a guarantee protecting the skier's investment. The best guarantee the skis for up to three years. Naturally these advantages result in increased prices (up to three times those of wooden jumpers), but the value may be well worth the expense.

Appropriately, all jumpers vary in length and the skier's selection is based on his height and weight.

THE JUMP POSITION

Before heading on to the water, the skier practices his "on the jump" stance. It is essential that he learn to *freeze* in this position on the approach to the jump.

In the freeze position for beginner jumpers, the skier is in a crouch position with knees and arms bent, head up, skis shoulder width apart with weight evenly distributed between them. The grip on the handle is the baseball grip. It is essential that the skier bend forward slightly from the waist with his weight on the balls of his feet.

This position is retained in the approach, on the ramp, and on the landing.

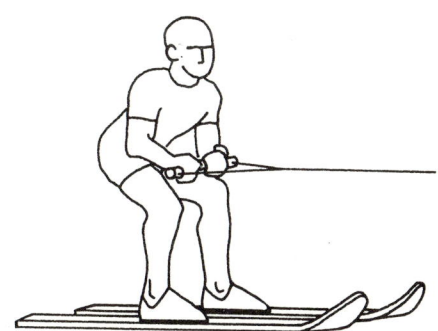

BOAT-SKIER PATH

The beginner jumper uses a *graduated side method* for his initial jump. This entails a different pattern for the driver and the skier.

The boat approaches the ramp at roughly a 30° angle. The boat is always on the right side of the jump, and the skier is on the left or ramp side of the boat. Boat speed for the beginner is approximately 22 miles per hour. This pattern for the beginner is retained throughout the beginning process, until the boat eventually runs parallel to the jump for the beginner's first *over the top* run. After each run, the skier must be reminded of the alteration in the next run and his corresponding change.

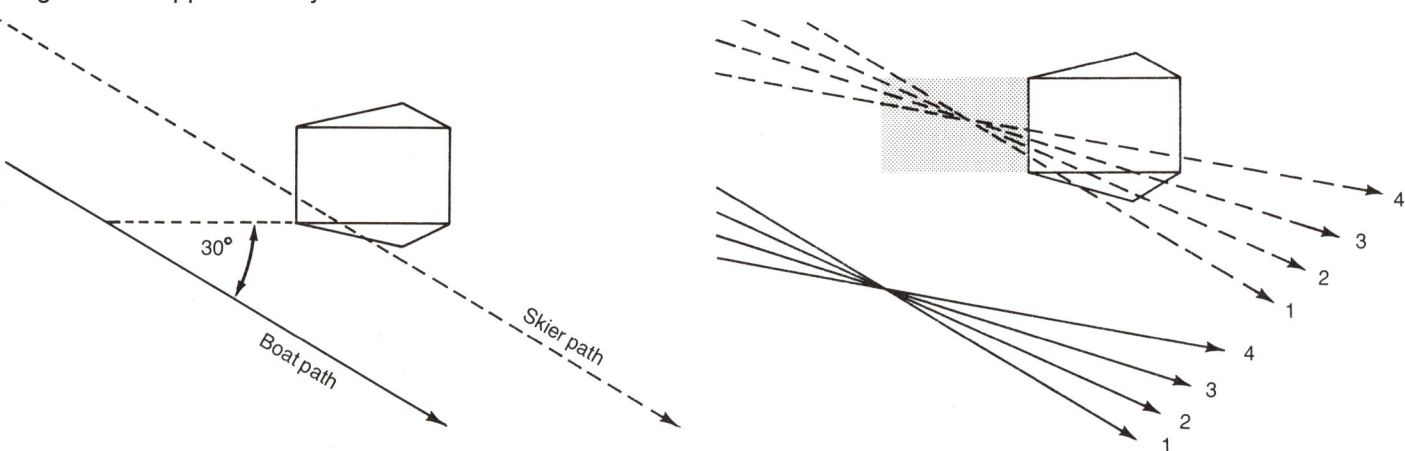

GRADUATED SIDE METHOD

The jump must be wet and set at 3 to 4 feet.

The skier takes a 5 minute run on the jumpers to get used to them and to practice the *crouch* position.

The skier starts by jumping over the lower corner of the jump, using correct body form, with the eyes looking towards the horizon. This allows the skier to gradually get used to the difference between skiing on the water and on the jump in terms of ski drag (the jump is much more slippery), and to get over the psychological barrier of *going over* a ramp. It also gives the observer in the boat the opportunity to watch and correct the skier's body position and stance before the skier advances to the next stage.

With a slight alteration in boat approach, the skier can now go off the ramp at a slightly higher level. Note the body position on the jump and the concentration on the horizon by the jumper. It is essential that the jumper hold on to the handle throughout the jumps. In the event of a fall, it will pull him clear of the jump.

It is also extremely important that the skis be flat on the jump or the result will be a loss of control on the jump, spreading skis and a sideways fall. If the skier approaches the jump in the freeze position from about 25 feet before the jump, there should be no problem.

In the final side attempt before the skier's *over the top* run, the observer checks the body position, making sure it is perfect before the skier attempts the straight run. The jump should be off the top side corner with the skier's knees and arms bent, head up and eyes looking at the horizon, body bent forward at the waist and weight evenly distributed on the balls of the feet.

Landings are easiest if the freeze position is maintained. They possess no more impact than jumping from a chair or table.

With the boat course altered such that the boat runs parallel to the jump and 15 to 20 feet away from its right side, the jumper has to swing to his left and approach the lower left corner of the ramp in the freeze position. If the skier

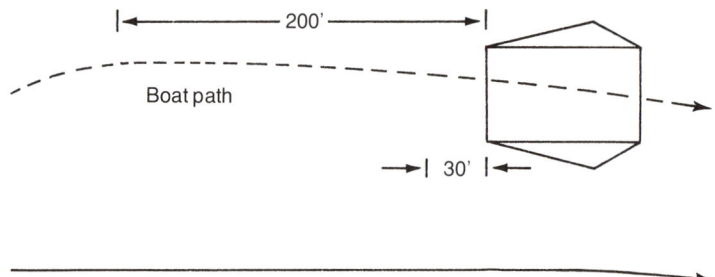

remembers to hold the freeze position, to hold on to the handle and to look up, the result will be favorable.

Aids to the Skier

- After a fall give the okay signal (hands clasped over the head) before recovering the skis.
- Go out before the run at the jump and accommodate yourself to the skis by cutting hard and by jumping wakes.
- Retain the freeze position throughout the jump, watching the horizon all the while.

ADVANCED JUMPING

Like all other aspects of the sport, it is best to break advanced jumping into stages, isolating the specific skills and developing each progressively.

Single-wake Cuts

After mastering the actual jumping feat, the skier concentrates on the cut towards the jump. This can be a gradual progression, with each successive jump being initiated from closer to the left wake. While the skier concentrates and freezes for the jump, he implements the characteristics of a good cut towards the ramp. This requires the weight to be back on the skis, head up, and the rope to be pulled in low to the hip region. The cut gradually develops from weak to strong with the emphasis on form throughout. The goal is a good form cut from between the wakes with maximum velocity attained through a strong pull and weight transfer.

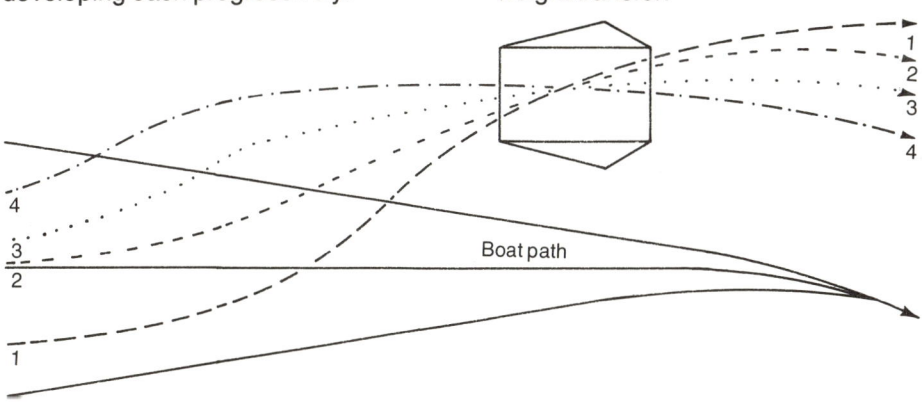

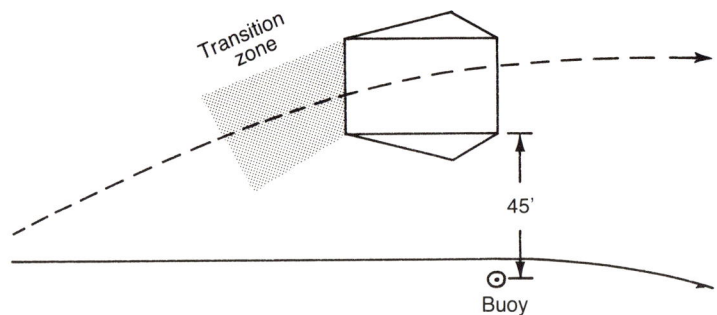

Transition Zone

The *transition phase* or *zone* is that 15 to 20 feet before the jump ramp where the skier changes from his cutting position to the freeze position. The size of the transition zone depends on the skier's reaction time in changing from the first position to the second.

The body position that the jumper will assume on the ramp is determined in the transition zone. The skier changes his position from shoulders and weight back with a strong pull to the forward ready or freeze position with the skis flat on the water ready for the jump. During this phase the jumper must exert full control. It is the most critical phase in jumping, and concentration must be maximized to succeed in the transition.

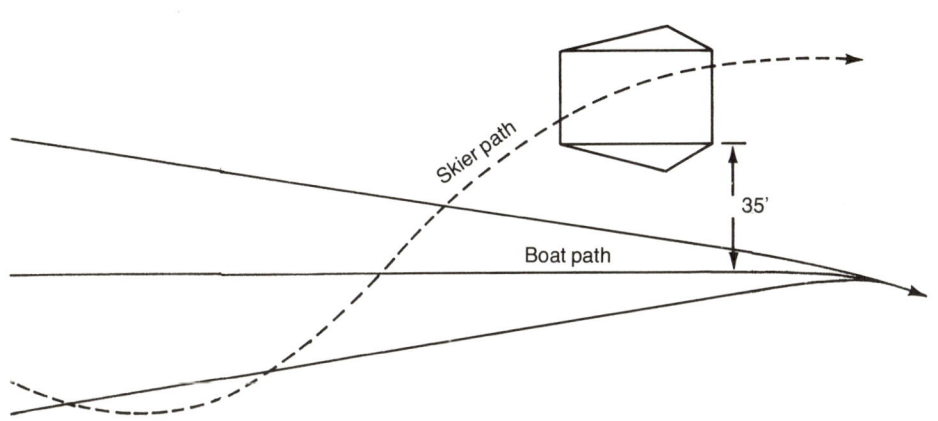

Popping

Popping is timing the extension of the legs to coincide with the skier reaching the crest at the top of the ramp. This produces a maximum vertical acceleration while minimizing the loss of the horizontal component. The result is an increase in jumping distance if the pop is executed at the proper moment from the proper stance (weight on the balls of the feet, shoulders ahead of the hips, head up, and knees over the insteps). Holding the arms straight and pulling in while on the jump results in additional distance. The pop is initiated while the skier is between the bottom and the middle of the jump if

Double-wake Cuts

The double-wake cut, an extension of the single-wake cut, provides the jumper with additional momentum towards the jump. The jumper starts out to the boat's left, swings over to the right and cuts hard towards the ramp. At the commencement of the cut, the weight is thrust back to the rear of the skis, a hard pull is exerted in to the hip, and the skier is concentrating on the jump. The purpose of the double-wake cut is to gather as much horizontal velocity as possible before the ramp.

the skier is travelling at a high speed, and later if his speed has been reduced.

A pop from the correct position, in which the weight is forward over the balls of the feet, results in more distance.

If the skier's weight is back, the vertical popping action reduces the possible distance by going against the horizontal velocity. To reduce the loss of the linear velocity, bring the weight forward.

The position on the ramp is determined in the transition zone before the jump. Obviously then, the components of a good popping action depend on the position of the skier there. The skier prepares for the pop off the ramp while he is in the transition phase.

In the Air

In the air the jumper uses the two-handed method of controlling the tow rope rather than the older one-hand

grasp. A two-handed grip of the handle provides the jumper with additional power and overall control throughout the jump. The body position is determined by the preceding stage; that is, the position of the body in the air is determined by the position on the ramp. In the air, the upper body is over the skis, legs and arms are straight and the skis are parallel to the surface of the water. Looking at the horizon will ensure that the jumper's head is up.

Landing

The skier retains his air position as closely as possible when landing. He brings the handle in towards his body to absorb any slack rope, and he absorbs the impact of the landing with his knees.

Bad landings could be the result of weak knees, which result in the skier crushing or folding on landing, or bad positioning in the air and on landing, so that when the body lands the centre of gravity is behind the feet and the skier folds backwards.

A few views on advanced jumping below the tournament level have been presented. The six skills should be reviewed and practiced independently and then gradually worked together to produce a better performance in jumping. For jumping beyond this level, it is best to approach a coach and follow his instruction.

Aids to the Skier

- Never indulge in marathon jumping. Set a maximum number of jumps per run at 4 or 5 and then rest.
- If you are going to be late setting for the jump or the body position is incorrect, throw the handle up and pass the jump by on the left side.

Jumping is exhilarating, but dangerous. Keep this in mind when you are approaching a six-foot ramp at speeds in excess of 55 miles per hour.

Chapter 7   Trick Skiing

Trick skiing is one of the most satisfying and motivating aspects of the sport. Once a skier has mastered his first trick on waterskis, his desire to master another, indeed all tricks, is increased tenfold.

Anyone can participate in trick skiing. A large boat and a large motor are not prerequisites. In fact, the maximum boat speed required is roughly 20 mph.

Boat

The novice can sometimes start his tricking behind a boat as small as an 18 HP. It is an asset, however, to have a unit which throws a relatively large wake for the more advanced wake tricks. It is also good to have a pylon in the center of the boat. This determines the angle of pull of the rope in relation to the skier. When the rope is placed higher in the boat, it is easier to perform tricks.

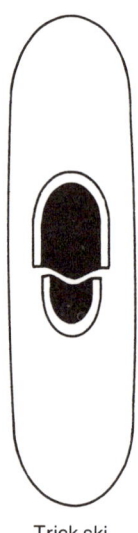

Trick ski

Skis

The next item of importance to the trick skier is the skis. The trick ski is between 39 and 44 inches in length and between 8 and 9-3/4 inches in width. The size depends on the skier's size and ability. Large skis do not slip easily on the water surface, *catch*, or ride high on the water.

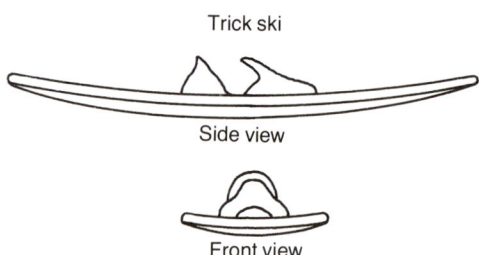

Length	Weight
39-41 inches	Less than 100 pounds
41-43 inches	100-170 pounds
44-46 inches	170 pounds plus

These measurements serve as only a guideline to the trick skier. Personal preference often determines the selection of a length for trick skis.

The shape of the trick ski differs drastically from that of the slalom, jumpers, or beginner's pairs. They are rockered along the longitudinal plane in an arc similar to the arc of a circle and they have no keel. Both these features facilitate turning the skis through 360° while on the water. Trick skis are designed to slide on the surface of the water with minimal opposition or friction.

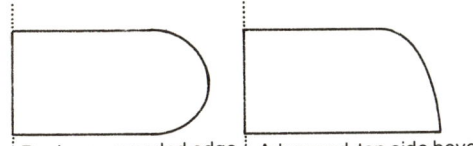
Beginner–rounded edge | Advanced–top side bevel

Edges on trick skis are important. For the beginner, the edges are slightly rounded. This permits a slight amount of cheating on turns, making the rudiments of the basic trick easier. Rounded edges are less likely to catch an edge, thus downing a skier. The accomplished trick skier uses skis which have a sharp edge and a reverse bevel design. The beveled edge is on the top of the ski and the action is opposite to that of the slalom ski. The ski is kept *on top* of the water. If an edge should catch some water, the dihedral effect of the bevel takes over, causing the ski edge to lift out of the water, and saves the skier from an impending fall. A slalom ski with the bevel on the bottom edge is sucked into the water. The reverse occurs here because the bevel is on the top of the ski. The beveled edge is especially functional in control and performance during wake turns.

Trick skis are made from either wood or fiberglass. Both are excellent values, depending on the skier's preference. Fiberglass skis offer several benefits not provided by wooden skis. They are as much as 30 or 40 per cent lighter in some cases, and they give the skier more freedom of movement and more speed. Some glass skis have a rubber-type edge, a definite boon to the novice since many times during the learning stage a new skier bangs the edges. This results in chips, bruises, and the like and ultimately in a reduced performance of the ski. As with glass jumpers and slaloms, the inter-ski difference (difference between pairs) is reduced through computer design and manufacture. Guarantees are generally liberal. Of prime importance, during the off-season the fiberglass ski retains its shape, especially its rocker.

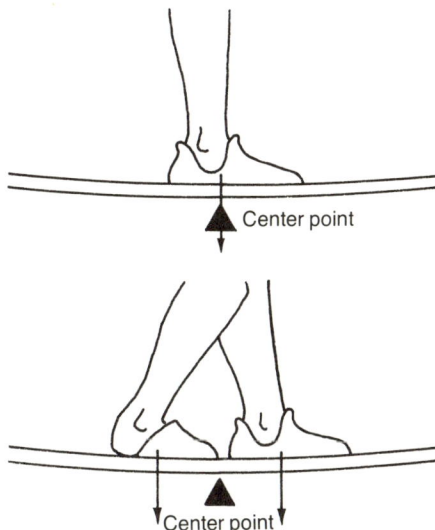

Bindings

Bindings on a trick ski should be center mounted (i.e., at the fulcrum point of the ski). Some skiers mount one ski binding ahead of the center point and then mount a rear toepiece immediately behind it. The theory is that this will place the center of gravity over fulcrum point of the ski when the skier is on one ski. This is not necessary as the net effect is almost inconsequential when skiing on one ski.

Trick ski with rear toepiece

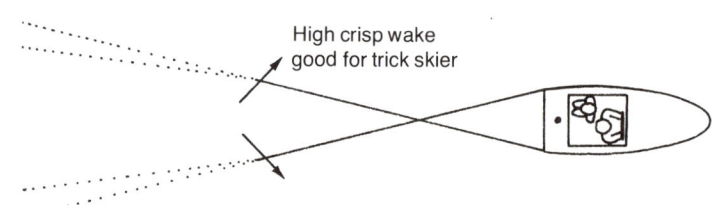

High crisp wake good for trick skier

It can, however, affect the skier's performance of tricks while skiing on two skis since one foot will be ahead of the other. Personal preference is the skier's guide. More than on any other ski, the bindings on a trick ski should fit so snuggly that the ski becomes an extension of the leg. When mounting a rear toepiece, keep it as close as possible to the front foot heel. Before drilling holes indiscriminately, take a few runs on the single trick ski and experiment with rear foot placement, trying different angles. Secure the most comfortable and stable angle and place the rear toepiece accordingly. Both feet must fit completely on the ski.

Some experienced trick skiers do not use a rear toepiece. They prefer to apply a strip of a non-slide, rubberized material on which they can place their foot. The skier requires time to remove and replace the foot in a binding during a trick run (there is also a degree of difficulty associated with insertion) whereas no such problems exist with the skidless strip. In competition, where a trick run is 20 seconds long, a lost second can mean the loss of valuable points.

Towrope

The length of the towrope used in trick skiing differs from that used in slalom or jumping. Normal towlines are roughly 75 feet in length. The trick skier uses a line which brings him in closer to the boat, in the area where the wake is considerably higher, usually near the V made by the wakes meeting. This means, depending on the boat, that the rope will be between 35 and 50 feet long and is usually 3/8 inch in diameter. This extra thickness reduces the elastic effect of the normal rope.

Handle

The trick handle is a slightly longer one than slalom handles to ensure ease of handling during tricks. Accompanying the handle is a toehold device. The beginner tricker should have a *sling*. It provides a secure grip for the skier but it does not grasp the skier so tightly that his foot won't come out. The beartrap is an extension of the sling toehold. An advanced skier who is extremely stable on one foot uses this type of link with the boat. The beartrap locks the foot into the rope, thereby reducing the necessity for the skier to concentrate on the towrope foot. A competent driver is a necessity for a skier doing toehold tricks. A fall must be immediately recognized, and the boat must stop or the skier will be pulled and he may tear a muscle.

Wetsuit

Because of its buoyancy, the wetsuit is a valuable aid for the trick skier. At speeds between 12 and 20 mph, the fall impact is relatively slight, and the boat can return to a fallen skier quickly. In this case, it is not necessary to wear a jump jacket, which might hamper the performance of an accomplished skier.

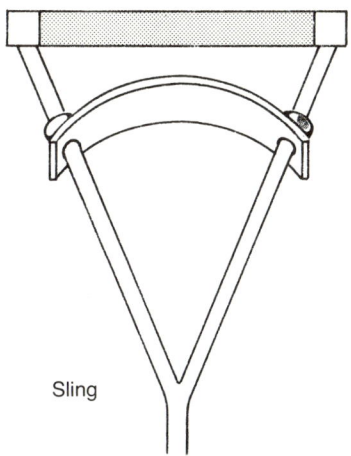

Sling

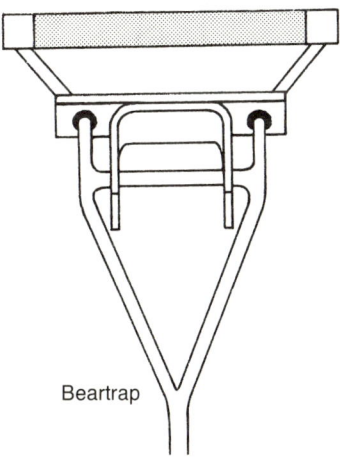

Beartrap

DRY-LAND PRACTICE

As with other aspects of water skiing, rehearse on dry land those activities which are to be performed on water. In trick skiing, it is especially important to learn to move and handle the rope and skis in addition to learning the body action.

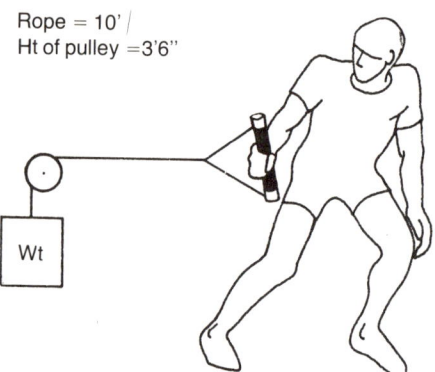

Rope = 10'
Ht of pulley = 3'6"
Wt

Hook up a rope to a weighted pulley system on dry land and practice without skis the first time through. The pulley should approximate the pull of a boat. Concentrate on how to move the rope throughout the course of the trick. Keep the handle in close to the body. Repeat this as often as necessary, slowly at first, then quickly, until it is mastered. Run through the trick again, concentrating on body, leg and foot action. Keep it as close as possible to a simulated water demonstration and retain body form. Finally, with the skis on and using an old piece of carpet or some similar substance on the dock, run through the trick completely. Concentrate on good overall form and attain a high level of proficiency before trying the trick on water.

Time spent on dry land is not wasted. It is a necessary prerequisite to doing a trick on water and it saves time and fuel.

Aids for the Skier

When doing tricks on land or on water:
- Keep the head up at all times. Never look down.
- Keep the body vertical and as close to perpendicular to the water surface as possible. A straight body decreases the time spent in a spin or turn.
- Develop a trick rhythm (an up and down bobbing motion) and use this in the tricks.
- Use the *upweighting* effect when tricking. When upweighting the skis, do not lift them off the surface of the water or land. The pressure is simply removed or reduced in the turn.
- Keep the handle low and into the body whenever tricking. This is one of the secrets of a good trick skier.
- Use an overhand grip on the long handle and turn naturally, inverting the hand in the spin around (knees are flexed).
- Lead into tricks with your head and shoulders but take care not to lead with the head too much or over-controlling will result.

WATER PRACTICE

A run of ten minutes is a good initiation to the trick skis. They are exceedingly slippery on the water. Control them by using the edges. Practice cutting hard and popping off the top of wakes. Make controlled landings. In short, familiarize yourself with the action of the trick skis before trying any tricks.

BOAT SPEED

When tricking, boat speed usually ranges between 12 and 20 miles per hour. This depends on factors such as ski size, skier's weight, and personal preference. However, find the speed at which you can best trick ski, and the driver records this for successive runs. Ski directly behind the boat and have the speed adjusted so that it just exceeds the point at which the skis plane. That is, do not let the skis sink into a wall of froth. Keep them atop the water and moving freely.

BASIC TRICKING

While skiing behind the boat, the prospective tricker assumes a basic tricker's stance. The knees are bent and flexed allowing the skier to keep a bouncing rhythm. Arms are slightly bent and held low towards the hips. The back is straight and the head up.

Sideslide (90°)

As with all tricks, this one is performed on the dock first. The 180° turn can be learned first if the 90° turn is too difficult.
The arms are extended and held low to the hip region (this keeps the center of gravity low and reduces the tendency of the rope to pull the skier over). At the start of the turn, pull the rope in with a steady applied pressure until the hands reach the hip. Release the handle with the outside or back hand. The turn should be a complete 90°, not a half-turn. Go all the way.

The knees are close together and the edges of the skis, those farther away from the boat, are set.

As the turn is completed, the body is at right angles to the boat's path with the head up, the body straight, the angled arm holding the bar in low to the hip, and the other arm extended out for balance.
At the beginning of the turn, use the bouncing or upweighting action. It enables the skis to slide around with reduced resistance to the water.

71

One-eighty Turn (180°) Front-to-Back

The next step is a 180° turn. This is a critical phase in the mastery of trick skiing as it is the basis for learning how to ski backwards.

Continue the rhythmic bouncing or upweighting motion as the turn is initiated. Maintain a steady two-handed pull in to the body. If trouble develops, continue the pull, as you rotate, until the hands or arms break across the stomach region.

At this point release the hand farther away from the boat.
Keeping the handle in close to the body, allow an inward (towards the body) rotation of the handle and arm.

If the handle is close to the body, it can easily be located with the free hand.

Skiing Backwards

A good trick skier must be as adept at skiing backwards as frontwards. Practice skiing backwards, using edge control and crossing both wakes until you have fully accommodated to the skis and the novel sensation of going backwards.

If done correctly, the wrist and the hand holding the handle will touch the lower back region with palms facing away from the body.

The turn need not be rapidly executed; a constant rhythmic upweighting turn free from a jerking rope pull is easiest. As with all tricks, keep the head up and do not look at the water or the skis.

In the final position, knees are slightly bent, and the back and head are straight and in line. Shift the body weight to the balls of the feet, and lean a little away from the boat. The handle is in close to the body and the wrists touch the small of the back.

One-eighty Back-to-Front

The 180° BF is a reverse of the 180° front-to-back. It is a simple natural action in which the skier releases one hand from the handle and allows the boat to pull him around. Grasp the handle as you reach the front position, and again, keep the head up.

Once both the 180s (front-to-back and back-to-front) have been learned, practice turning both ways. That is, learn to turn backwards by going either to the right or to the left, and complement this by returning to the front skiing position either way. A good tricker is equally good to both sides.

Three-sixty Turn (360°)

As the 180° is a continuation of the 90°, so the 360° is an extension of the 180° turn. In short, it is a rapid combination of the 180° front-to-back and the 180° back-to-front. To learn the 360°, start as in a 180° position and continue to the back position. Initially, make a short pause at the back position before continuing around to the front. After becoming more accustomed to the turning action involved, eliminate the pause and make the 360° turn one continuous move.

Remember to keep the head up, to keep the rope in close to the body, and to initiate the turn with an upweighting motion while pulling in evenly on the rope.

Wake 180° Front-to-Back

Having mastered all of the preceding tricks the next trick to learn is a wake 180°, which is very much like a surface 180° only it is done in the air after leaving the crest of the boat wake. As the height of the wake is a factor, use the highest, cleanest portion of the wake available.

The proper length rope is a necessity. Rope control is especially important in wake tricks. For ease in doing wake tricks, keeping the handle in close to the body is an absolute necessity.

While competitively frowned on, *cheating* helps in mastering the wake 180° turn. This is achieved by going from inside the wake to the outside of the boat's wake on the side which proves easiest for the 180° turn (i.e., if the skier turns the 180° best going left, then he uses the wake to his left).

When coming to the top of the wake, pull in steadily on the rope with two hands, as in the 180° turn, and lead with shoulders and head into the turn. Complete the 180° turn without going off the water surface. Hold the handle close to the body. On the first attempts, do not *pop*; get used to the body positions and especially to the rope handling. Later, start to pop by

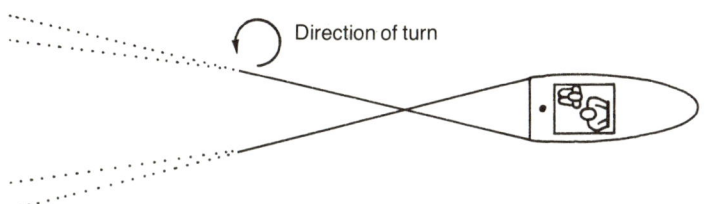

Direction of turn

Wake 180° Back-to-Front

This is a naturally executed trick. Simply release the hand on the outside of the rotation as you pop off the wake. The boat's pull helps the skier complete the turn as he lands in skiing position (knees bent, head up, back straight, and arms slightly bent). The keys are erect body position, control of rope position, and keeping the head up.

straightening the legs from a crouch position at the crest of the wake. Complete the turn as you land on the other side of the wake and set the edges of the skis for stability and absolute control.

Learn to go off both wakes with the 180° turn, and then learn the trick going from outside to inside the wake. In either case, it is not necessary to make a frantic rushing cut at the wake. The key to the success of the trick is an approach of 2 to 3 feet and a popping at the crest of the wake for extra lift. Good body position (straight body with head back, hips and knees in line) is essential as it partially determines the speed at which the rotation can occur.

Wake 360°

The wake 360° should be developed next. Implementation of a technique called a *wrap* will initially aid in the completion of the trick.

Start by doing an ordinary 360° behind the boat. If the rotation is to occur to the right, then place the right arm behind the back and grasp the handle.

The handle is pulled in low by the left hand such that the opposite hand can easily grasp it without a loss of body control.

This free hand then releases the handle and grasps the rope further ahead for stability. The skier is now in a wrap position. Note the body and head position.

Next, release the front hand from the rope, upweight and let the boat and rope pull you around to the front skiing position. When first learning this trick, the turn need not be a rapid spin. The major emphasis is on learning how to handle the rope.

Stepovers

The final two-ski trick which should be attempted by the novice is a stepover. As the name implies, it is basically a 180° front-to-back or back-to-front in which the skier steps over the tow-rope while he is turning.

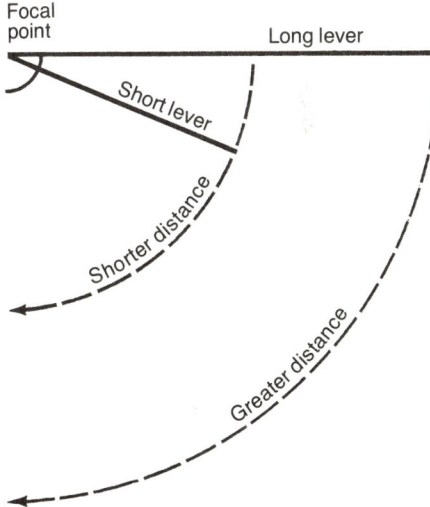

As with the wake 180°, progress outwards to the crest of the wake. Do not leave the water's surface before popping from the crest. The trick is done in the air.

Key points to remember in doing this trick:
- Keep the rope close into the body and as close to the hip region as possible.
- Keep the body perfectly straight while popping off the wake (to increase *spin* ability—a necessity in more difficult tricks).

The key here is the action of the leg which passes over the rope. The knee *must* be bent in as closely to the body as is anatomically possible. This produces two significant results. Since the ski is in close to the body, a skier can exert control over it and its actions. More important, a bent leg reduces the amount of work actually done by the skier. If a skier attempts to do the stepover with a straight leg, he will be forced to move a greater weight through a greater arc distance. With the leg in tight, work is reduced and maximum control results.

As with all tricks, keep the trunk straight. Obviously the rope cannot be lowered to water level since to do this a skier would have to bend from the waist. Keep the back and body perpendicular to the water throughout. Hold the rope with two hands at roughly crotch level. As you upweight or bounce upward, pull in steadily on the rope.

Initiate the turn by lifting the outside ski up and into the body. Flexion of the ankle will ensure that the tip of the ski is in correct position as it follows the knee's lead over the rope.

The ski is placed on the water, enabling the skier to ski comfortably backwards. Later he might use a single-hand method but initially he uses both hands on the handle.

As with other tricks, return to the front skiing position. Possibly the back-front stepover is a good way to learn stepovers if the skier is timid. Learn the tricks to both sides, turning both right and left.

Since the leg action is essential to the success of the trick, special dry-land practice should be used. Use of a crotch level table, saw-horse, or even a hurdle allows the skier to practice lifting the leg over the rope, under control, as in the turns. Extensive dry-land practice should precede any water attempts.

Two-Ski Backwards Start

While learning to ski backwards, learn to start backwards.

Basically an easy trick to master, start in the water facing the boat with head up, arms straight, and knees bent (beginner's position). As the rope draws taut, do a 180° turn in the water, rolling over on the stomach so that the back ski tips are up out of the water.

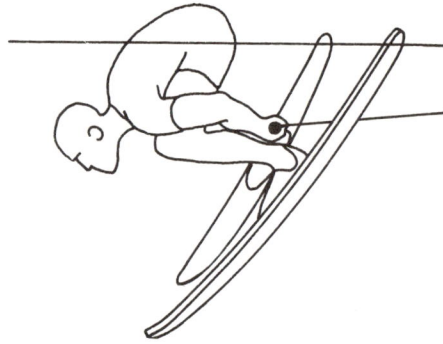

Knees are kept bent up to the chest, and both arms are extended behind with both hands gripping the handle below the buttocks.

When ready to accelerate, dunk the head into the water and maintain this position until the driver has accelerated.

Coming out of the water, assume the back skiing position by standing up and raising the handle up to the small of the back. Keep the head up and look away from the water.

Further two-ski tricks can be learned, and, as can be expected, they all progress towards the upward end of the difficulty range. The novice trick skier should seek the assistance of an experienced instructor when learning these sequences.

Having mastered the novice level, you may wish to attempt some more ski tricks. Install a rear heel piece or a patch of non-skid material on the ski. Many of the same tricks learned on two skis can also be done on a single ski.

One-Ski 90°

The one-ski 90° is almost identical to the two-ski sideslide in that the head is up, the handle is low to the hips and the knees are bent. In the bouncing motion, be sure to turn a full 90°. Weight is evenly distributed on both legs. The key to success in the one-ski sideslide is the use of the rear foot which controls the angulation of the edges of the ski.

One-Ski 180°

This trick may be one of the more difficult for the beginning tricker because it requires almost perfect weight distribution. Key points in mastering this turn are:
- Keep the body straight and angled away from the boat slightly more than in two-ski tricks.
- Keep the weight slightly ahead of the center of gravity of the ski and keep the feet close together.
- Use the same rope control and upweighting techniques as before.

Once skiing backwards on one ski and good control of one-ski turns have been learned, mastery of the other one-ski tricks (360°, wake turns, and stepovers) will be easier.

Wake turns must be executed flawlessly. Be particular about the body position and the upweighting. Avoid a rushing cut at the wake to attain height.

When doing stepovers, keep the knee bent in close to the body, and touch the toe to the water after stepping over the rope.

Toehold Tricks

A final group of tricks are the toehold tricks. The beginning tricker should use a sling-type harness as opposed to the beartrap used by many experienced skiers.

Toe 180° Front-to-back. With the foot comfortably in the toe sling, hold the rope low to the water with the leg bent. The ski leg is also bent and the trunk erect. Arms are extended for balance and the head is up.

While turning, rotate the handle leg to the inside (towards the midline of the body). Keep this leg bent at all times. It is the link with the boat and acts as a shock absorber.

Toe 180° Back-to-front. The keys to the successful tow 180° back-to-front are as follows:
- Keep the head up and the back arched as far back as comfortably possible. The arms are extended for balance.
- The handle leg is bent at the knee and initially faces the rear. As you turn, upweight with a small hop and pull the handle down and in towards the other foot. In completing the turn, allow the handle leg to extend forward towards the boat, but keep it bent.

The accompanying charts show other tricks skiers can try once the ones described have been mastered. At each stage, however, stress perfection of form and fluid movement. These are essential in becoming a good tricker. If possible, get an experienced instructor to work with you, both on land and on the water.

Once a few tricks have been learned, a skier might want to put them together in a sequence as competitive trick skiers do. Competitive *runs* are 20 seconds long, and each skier gets two runs. Points are awarded each trick as per the chart. While a beginner's run may not include 15 or 16 tricks as a top competition skier's does, it can provide a skier with a tremendous feeling of accomplishment and self-satisfaction.

		Water Turns					Wake Turns			
		2 Skis		1 Ski			2 Skis		1 Ski	
	No.	Basic	Reverse	Basic	Reverse	No.	Basic	Reverse	Basic	Reverse
Side Slide	1	20	20	70	70		—	—	—	—
Slide Slide Toehold	2	—	—	150	230		—	—	—	—
180 F-B	3	30	30	60	60	14	50	50	80	80
B-F	4	30	30	60	60	15	50	50	80	80
360 F-F	5	40	40	90	100	16	110	110	150	150
B-B		40	40	90	100	17	160	160	210	210
540 F-B		50	—	110	—	18	240	240	310	310
B-F		50	—	110	—	19	250	250	320	320
720 F-F		60	—	130	—	20	260	—	320	—
B-B		60	—	130	—	21	300	—	350	—
180 F-B Stepover	6	80	80	120	—	22	110	110	180	—
B-F Stepover	7	70	70	110	—	23	110	110	160	—
360 F-F Stepover		—	—	—	—	24	200	200	260	260
B-B Stepover		—	—	—	—	25	200	200	260	260
540 B-F Stepover		—	—	—	—	26	270	290	370	370
F-B Stepover		—	—	—	—	27	240	240	340	370
180 F-B Toehold	8	—	—	100	110	28	—	—	150	180
B-F Toehold	9	—	—	120	130	29	—	—	180	180
360 F-F Toehold	10	—	—	220	300	30	—	—	300	350
B-B Toehold	11	—	—	250	280	31	—	—	330	330
540 F-B Toehold	12	—	—	400	400	32	—	—	500	—
B-F Toehold	13	—	—	400	—	33	—	—	500	—
180 F-B Toehold Stepover		—	—	—	—	34	—	—	290	—
B-F Toehold Stepover		—	—	—	—	35	—	—	320	—
Somersault		—	—	—	—	36	450	—	450	—

By permission of the Canadian Water Ski Association.

DESCRIPTION	TRICK NO.	WATER TURNS 2 SKIS Basic	Rev.	1 SKI Basic	Rev.	TRICK NO.	WAKE TURNS 2 SKIS Basic	Rev.	1 SKI Basic	Rev.	TRICK NO.	RAMP TURNS 2 SKIS Basic	Rev.	1 SKI Basic	Rev.
180° FB	1	30	30	60	60	14	50	50	80	80	37	90		150	
180° BF	2	30	30	60	60	15	50	50	80	80		90		150	
360° FF	3	40	40	90	100	16	110	110	150	150		130		250	
360° BB		40	40	90	100	17	160	160	210	210		130		250	
Each Additional 180°		10		20											
540° FB						18	240	240	310	310					
540° BF						19	250	250	320	320					
720° FF						20	290		350						
720° BB						21	300		350						
Stepover 180° FB	4	80	80	120		22	110	110	180		38	160		230	
Stepover 180° BF	5	70	70	110		23	110	110	160		39	130		200	
Stepover 360° FF						24	200	200	260	260					
Stepover 360° BB						25	180	180	240	240					
Stepover 540° FB						26	240		340						
Stepover 540° BF						27	240		340						
Toehold 180° FB	6			100	110	28			150	180					
Toehold 180° BF	7			120	130	29			180	180					
Toehold 360° FF	8			220	220	30			300	300					
Toehold 360° BB	9			250	250	31			330	330					
Toehold 540° FB	10			400	400	32			500						
Toehold 540° BF	11			400		33			500						
T'hold-S'over 180° FB						34			290						
T'hold-S'over 180° BF						35			320						
Side Slide	12	20	20	70	70						40	250		380	
Air SS and SS Ldg.												230		350	
Toehold SS-2.0 Sec.	13			300	380										
Toehold SS-1.5-1.9 Sec.				180	200										
Toehold SS (short interval)				120	150										
Somersault						36	450		450		41	430		570	
Air 180° FB											42	120		180	
Air 180° BF												120		180	
Air 360° FF												210		310	
Air 360° BB												210		310	

From the AWSA 1972-1973 Tournament Rules.
By permission of the American Water Ski Association.

Chapter 8 Barefoot Skiing

EQUIPMENT

The equipment needed for barefooting is usually already in the ski shack. The first essential is a boat capable of pulling a skier at least 34 miles per hour, although a speed of 40 miles per hour is generally preferable. The skier who is going to barefoot should be going at a minimum of 34 miles per hour when he steps off, or he might experience a sinking action.

The second necessary piece of equipment is a jump jacket. In barefooting some hard falls occur, and anything that might cushion these falls is an asset. It is also desirable to have a wetsuit, or at least a pair of shorty jump pants (wetsuit pants or rubber pants).

Prior to barefooting, the skier must attain sufficient speed while being supported by a ski of some sort. The ideal step-off ski is a slalom ski with the front heel piece removed. The ski must be devoid of any sharp objects. If sharp objects can't be removed before attempting barefooting, use another ski.

A final piece of equipment is an extra 30 to 50 feet of rope attached to a standard 75 foot length of rope. The added rope removes the skier from the rough water or froth caused by the outboard and places him in calm water.

Barefoot Speeds	
Weight of Skier	**Boat Speed**
220 lbs.	42 mph
210 lbs.	41 mph
200 lbs.	40 mph
190 lbs.	39 mph
180 lbs.	38 mph
170 lbs.	37 mph
160 lbs.	36 mph
150 lbs.	35 mph
140 lbs.	34 mph
130 lbs.	33 mph
120 lbs.	32 mph
110 lbs.	31 mph
100 lbs.	30 mph

DRY-LAND PRACTICE

Dry-land practice is essential to learning barefooting and should be mastered before attempting it on the water.

Assume the standard slalom skiing position on the dock with the rope being held by the assistant/instructor.

When there is a great deal of tension on the rope, remove the back foot from the ski and place it about 8 inches from the ski and slightly in front of the other foot.
Plant the heel firmly on the dock or practice surface and point the toes up and inward.
Hold the handle with the baseball grip at about waist height throughout the run.
With the rope low and the first heel planted in the water (dock), gradually move to a sitting position and transfer about 80 per cent of the weight on to the free foot.
When most of the weight is over this foot, quickly remove the other foot from the step-off ski and plant it firmly in the water, heel first, with the toes pointed up and inward.

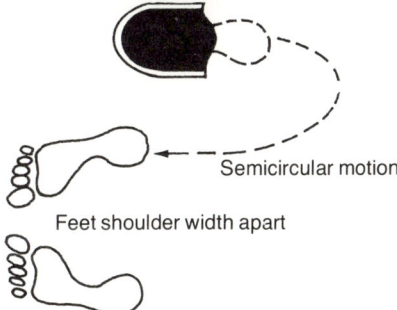

Freeing the foot from an open-backed binding.

Free yourself from the step-off ski with a slightly circular motion and a push to the outside.
When up in correct position, the weight is well back and the rope is at waist level.

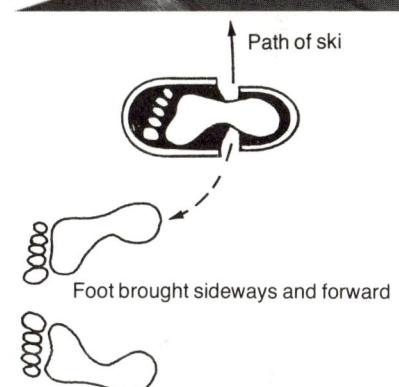

Freeing the foot from a binding with a heel piece.

Feet are about shoulder width apart, slightly pidgeon-toed, and the toes are pointing up.
Practice planting the foot with the toes up and put the heel in hard and quickly. A hard forward fall can hurt at this speed.

WATER PRACTICE

There are two methods for the beginner to stepoff. The first is especially useful in areas where many boats are running or where water conditions are choppy. It is preferable, however, to choose calm water for the first attempts.

Method One

Using a long rope, 100 to 125 feet, start out behind the boat and off the right side of the center wash if you are a right-footed slalom skier (left side for left-footed slalom skiers) where the water is calmest. It is a good idea to have some prearranged signals with the instructor so he can signal the skier to sit back further or move forward as necessary.

Follow the steps which were run through on the dock. Signal the driver to accelerate to the prearranged speed. Shift back to the sitting position with the head up and the rope held low, arms slightly bent.

Plant the free heel in the water in front of the other foot and gradually transfer the weight to it.

When most of the weight is on the barefoot, kick off the ski and immediately plant the ski foot beside the other.

Keep the weight back and the toes up. A forward fall could be caused by several factors. These include having the weight too far forward allowing the boat to pull the skier over, holding the rope too high, or planting the toes in the water.

As you get up on your feet, straighten the back and the legs. Proficient barefoot skiers straighten the legs completely and gradually move the weight forward, thereby reducing the spray. The easiest way to end a barefoot run is to toss the rope well away and sit back in the water. This is the safest and easiest method of finishing a run.

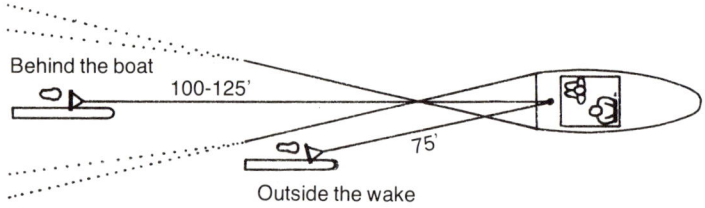

Method Two

This method requires the normal length rope. The barefooter assumes the same position, and everything is done exactly as in Method One except that the skier is to the outside of the wake instead of behind the boat. Again, right-footed slalom skiers go to the immediate right side of the wake, just where the calm water exists, while left-footers proceed to the other side. From here, everything is duplicated.

ADVANCED STARTS

Alternate methods of starting have been developed for the experienced barefoot skier. The jumpout barefoot is accomplished by a skier using ordinary pairs skis. It is best to use the extended rope (100 to 125 feet long) and to perform the start behind the boat.

Use ordinary pairs skis with the bindings looser than usual.
Signal the driver to accelerate to a speed of approximately 40 mph.
Assume a squat position with knees bent and head up.

When the boat accelerates, hop up and lift the feet out of the skis. The key to this method is the hop out of the skis. Great height does not necessarily need be attained for the start.
With the feet freed of the skis, straighten the legs forward, putting the weight back.

When the feet hit the water, they should be in barefoot position, slightly wider than shoulder width apart, with the toes up. Keep the rope low at this point and the arms well bent at impact to absorb the shock incurred in the action.

On impact, the skier may hit the water with the buttocks and then bounce forward slightly.
When landing, keep the legs straight, dig in with the heels, keep arms bent and hold the rope low, and keep the weight well back.

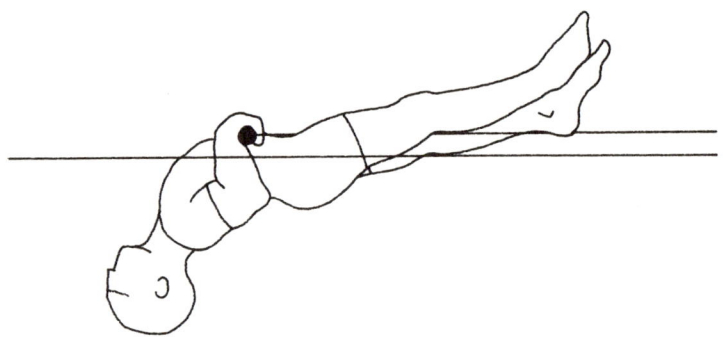

Another method of starting to barefoot is to start in deep water. This is more complicated and requires a more powerful boat.

The skier is in the water holding the handle tight to the center of the chest. When tension is exerted on the rope, cross the feet over the rope and lie back in the water.

The action of the boat pulls the lower torso out of the water and sinks the upper body. To compensate, arch the back and neck as much as possible. If the neck is not arched, a great deal of water may find its way up the nasal cavity and exert extreme pressure. Hyperextension of the neck creates a pocket which lessens this effect.

As soon as the skier drops his head back, the driver accelerates rapidly.

As the boat planes out, the skier with his legs still crossed over the rope will be in the sitting position, in effect, skiing on his buttocks.

Uncross the feet while planing on the buttocks and, keeping the rope low to the chest and arms bent, plant both feet (in some cases it is easier to plant first one foot and then the other immediately after) in the water. The skier is up and skiing barefoot.

If it is necessary to release the rope, uncross the legs and throw the handle up.

Caution. This is a start for experienced skiers who are good swimmers. It is also desirable for skiers to leave off the jump jacket or wear it beneath the wetsuit since the pressure exerted by the water sometimes has a drag or negative effect. In addition, jump jackets have been known to slide under the extreme pressure, causing serious injury to the barefooter's neck. Do not attempt this trick without a tight wetsuit or protective pants.

A barefooter can perform such tricks as one-foot barefoot, tumble turns, crossing wakes, and toehold barefoot.
Wake crossing is achieved in much the same fashion as it is on two skis. Simply lean in the direction in which you wish to go. Lifting first one foot, then the other, over the wake.
It is essential to keep the weight back and to keep the legs straight while going over the wake. Small wakes can be crossed without even lifting the feet. Just place the weight farther back.

Toehold barefoot is for experts only. One must be adept at both toehold tricking and barefooting.
From the barefoot position, lower the handle with both hands and keep the weight back.
Raise the toe straight up and insert into the beartrap making sure not to cross the midline of the body with the lead leg.
Slowly release the handle, transferring the pull to the foot from the hands. Do not let it snap or it will jerk you forward. Straighten the body slowly, moving the hands for balance.
In a fall, tuck to avoid injury.

Barefooting has proven to be a great act for ski show enthusiasts. Acts featuring barefooting include some of the starts mentioned as well as turnarounds, or even backwards barefooting. When barefooting, make sure capable people are on hand to assist you if necessary. A capable observer can avert serious injury to the barefooter.

Chapter 9 Kite Skiing

Though not actually waterskiing, kiting has been closely allied with the sport and has gained immensely in popularity in recent years. Being a proficient skier is not a necessity for becoming a good flier. In fact, non-skiers can learn to fly as well. For the purpose of this book, kiting will be assumed to be a specialized form of waterskiing.

Kiting is divided into two basic groups—gull wing kiting and flat kite flying.

Gull wing kites, which originated somewhere around 1945 and have been tested in association with the U.S.A. space capsule re-entry, can be considered a type of glider aircraft capable of flight independent of a boat or towline. In fact, in most cases, there is nothing either the boat driver or observer can do. The flier is in complete control, implementing changes in the center of gravity below the kite (by changing the attitude of the bar).

Gull wing kites generally fly at high altitudes and have ascended up to 4,750 feet when towed by boat and 9,700 feet when towed by plane. It is

obvious that in addition to the sense of vertigo one attains when gull wing kiting, there is a measure of danger associated with it. For this reason, proper dry-land and short-rope instruction from an experienced and capable gull wing instructor is an *absolute necessity*. Trial and error flights are dangerous and unwarranted.

Care must be taken in the selection and maintenance of equipment. Gull wing kites should be constructed with extreme care, and only by professionals. Poor quality could result in a fatal accident.

No more will be discussed concerning gull wing kites. Instead, skiers are encouraged to learn from a professional.

The second type of kite skiing is flat kite flying. This is more prevalent than gull wing flight. Whereas gull wing flight is determined by the flyer and can be independent of the boat, a flat kite's altitude and flight is almost totally determined by the observer-throttle man. It is incapable of free flight.

It is interesting to note the comparison between features of the kites.

	Gull Wing		**Flat**
	Seat hung from an A-frame at pressure point of sail with trapeze bar immediately in front of flyer	Support	Detachable seat belt arrangement which circumvents the upper thigh and affixes to the midpoint of the trapeze
	Controlled by flyer's shifts of body; capable of independent flight	Flight determination	Controlled by boat velocity; incapable of independent flight
	Must be extremely careful to check preceding every flight for damage; must be repaired with precision	Maintenance	Easily repaired with replacement parts
	Must have experienced and capable instructor with an in-depth understanding of what is happening. This kite is a delicate instrument which should be handled with respect.	Safety	Safe if care is taken and the kite is properly maintained; flyer can learn on his own

EQUIPMENT

The boat should be powerful enough not only to get the skier up in the air, but to maintain his altitude. A good unit has at least 115 HP and is capable of speed in excess of 40 mph. The observer faces the rear, controlling the center-mounted throttles with his left hand and the *quick release* with his right. The driver concentrates on steering straight ahead. For flying, it is essential that the boat have a pylon firmly fastened to the craft.

The next essential for flying is a kite. Numerous makes are available, but care should be taken in their selection. Generally, flat kites can be utilized, unless in high level competition, for both tricks and slalom. A slalom kite has a 3-point bridle to which the boat rope attaches, a wide trapeze bar and a wide tail. The trick kite has a 4-point bridle.

The size of the kite depends on the:
- Weight of the flyer. A heavy flyer requires a larger kite surface area than a light flyer. The larger the kite, the slower the speed of the boat. It is dangerous for a heavy flyer to use a small kite because too much speed results. A small flyer should not fly a large kite because it is affected by gusts of wind.
- Speed and power of the boat. A heavy flyer who is using a small kite requires a fast powerful boat.
- Wind conditions. The wind speed determines altitude. Some heavy flyers cannot get enough lift on a calm day. Flying into the wind reduces the boat speed and/or the size of the kite needed.
- Type of flying. Tricks require a larger kite, which provides a stable support.

The perfect kite for a particular skier is one which takes these things into consideration, but compromises may be necessary. Follow the advice of a competent kite flyer and be guided by the manufacturer's suggestions when purchasing a kite. A good kite is composed of aircraft aluminum alloy bars combined with stainless steel hardware (*e.g.,* set screws, cotter pins), styrofoam floats and a proper sail. The

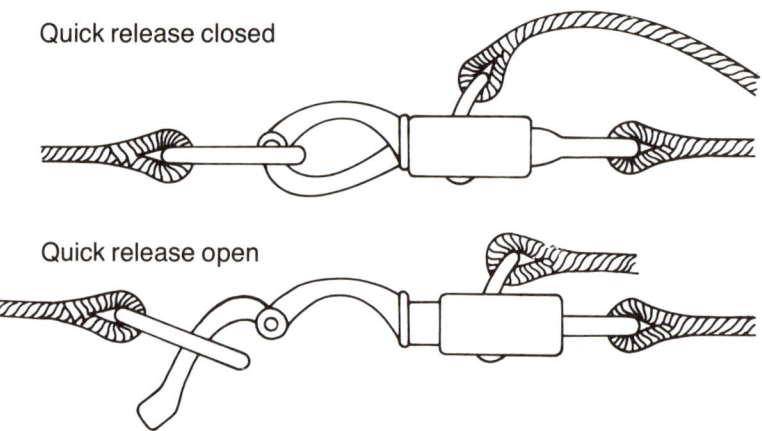

Quick release closed

Quick release open

trapeze bar in a good kite is really three bars, one inside the other. This maximizes the strength and durability of the bar and minimizes its weight.

The kite sail is usually of poly-coated nylon and comes complete with appropriate length ropes inside and out, such that the skier can complete the assemblage.

Before flying the kite, make sure it is assembled precisely as indicated by the accompanying instructions. Before the flights, double check the fittings to make sure they are taut. During the season and at the end of the season, check for worn ropes and replace them as soon as needed.

Accessories include 120 feet of 3/8-inch, wound or braided polypropyline rope, a quick release and a harness seat-belt arrangement which will support the flyer's weight from the trapeze bar. The harness is adjusted so that the skier's eyes are at bar level.

The quick release (QR) is an essential piece of safety equipment. It is attached to the pylon by a thick rope and the thin free rope goes to the hand of the observer. The ring end of the kite rope is placed in the QR. When the observer pulls the QR, the kite is released from the boat and floats downward. (Gull wing kites have similar releases except that they respond more readily under extreme tension.

As with all phases of skiing a jump jacket is worn. The importance of having three straps which go completely around the body is illustrated here. These jackets are placed under extreme pressure. The weight of the skier is often completely borne by the straps. A good jump jacket is essential.

In addition, for the sake of comfort and safety, a wetsuit or shorty pants are advisable.

DRIVING FOR KITING

Driving for the kite flyer requires a high degree of skill. When working with a beginning flyer, the driver steers directly into the wind, if any, and maintains a perfectly straight line. The driver never runs a beginner or novice downwind because the velocity of the boat is very high. At high speeds, control is reduced and a serious accident can occur. The man behind the wheel is responsible only for *steering* the boat.

The role of the observer in flat kite flying is critical. It is he who controls the success or failure of the kiter. The observer is responsible for:

- Controlling the altitude of the flyer. If he sees a flyer descending rapidly, he applies a steady, sharp forward throttle to get him back up. There is, however, a lag between the time of applied throttle and resultant upward motion of the kite.
- The safety of the flyer. With the assistance of the QR, the observer is responsible for *setting the flyer down* should the need arise. Such a case occurs when a flyer is in trouble and is apparently going to crash. The observer *pins* (releases) the flyer at the exact moment the flyer hits the water to prevent him being dragged upon impact. (This also saves the kite from damage.) It is also the job of the pin man to check out the flyer's equipment prior to flight; specifically, the QR hookup, the gas level, and the kite outfittings.
- Communicating with both driver and flyer. Preferably the observer is an experienced flyer, who is able to relate effectively to the man in the air by using agreed upon signals. Communication with the driver is verbal.
- Landing the flyer. The boat taxis the flyer into the dock area while the observer eases up on the throttle. As the flyer starts to sink slowly into the water, the observer pins him.

Kiting Signals

The basic signals used in flat kiting include the following:
- Spreading the legs in and out several times means the flyer wants more altitude (he wants more speed).
- Head shaking *no* means the flyer is uncomfortable and would like less altitude (boat speed slackens).
- Skis crossed at the front means the flyer wants to descend.

DRY-LAND PRACTICE

Put on the wetsuit and jump jacket, and adjust the skis (ordinary pairs or tricks). Slip into the harness, which accompanies the kite, making sure to tighten the straps around the thigh and to the outside, not into the crotch. Slide the free end of the harness through the lower two straps on the jump jacket, and knot those two straps to ensure that they won't slip out under pressure. The vest should fit snugly. Practice several times fastening and unfastening the harness to the kite.

Using a spare wing tip, paddle, or broom handle to simulate the motion of the kite, practice on land what will be done on the water. The attitude of the bar changes when weight is shifted to either side. To counter the movement of the bar, the beginning flyer should learn a shake method developed by the Summer Water Ski Services staff. Basically, this is a simple up and down motion of the trapeze bar used by the beginner if the kite starts to swing or oscillate. The observer can signal the novice by a simulated shake in the boat. Immediately following the shake, the beginner holds the bar level. Dry-land simulation of flight continues until the beginner's reactions are automatic.

With knowledge of what to do on the water and in the air, connect the harness to the kite and get two strong assistants to support the bar. Run through the following on the dock.

First, check the harness adjustment. When hanging freely from the bar, the eyes should be at bar level.

Second, check the thigh harnesses for comfort and adjust them if necessary.

Third, the bar and harness are more than capable of supporting a flyer's weight. Let go of the bar and assure yourself that it will. The kite will fly itself. All the flyer has to do is relax and stay in the center of the bar. Finally, the arms are placed wide on the trapeze and are relaxed. They bear none of the flyer's weight and act only as stabilizers. Keeping relaxed hands and arms on the trapeze bar avoids over-controlling the kite..

WATER PRACTICE

Water Start

The two-ski start with a kite is the same as the two-ski, deep-water start except that the flyer grasps a trapeze bar rather than a towbar handle. On the way out of the water, lift up on the bar to stop the drag on the kite. This is an easy task as the kite is light and partially raised by air pressure.

If it is difficult starting from the skis, start without skis on. This start is executed by lying in the water with the legs pointed back. As the kite rises out of the water, the flyer is lifted up immediately so that the water runs off the thighs and belly. With a little more power he is up and flying. Landing is achieved by the flyer letting his feet drag back and pushing the bar away as he is pinned.

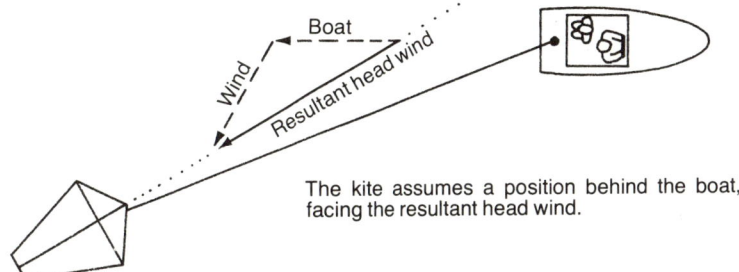

The kite assumes a position behind the boat, facing the resultant head wind.

Taxiing

Skiing with a kite is the same as with ordinary pairs. The kite will support itself while the flyer is skiing, but the flyer must ski when his skis are on the water.

While on the water, retain the body position in the center of the trapeze bar, and let the kite go where it wants. It is not necessary to ski behind the boat. The kite settles in a position behind the boat so that it is running in an *equilibrium* position determined by boat direction and wind direction.

Keep the arms relaxed and keep the eyes *constantly* on the observer in the boat.

Take-off

The flyer signals the observer when he is ready to take off by nodding his head. Keep the arms relaxed and let the harness bear the total weight. The arms are extended widely on the bars and slight pressure is applied to maintain a level bar.

If the kite starts to swing or oscillate, use two or three quick shakes. This allows some air to slip out of the sail, returns the trapeze bar to a normal attitude, and prevents over-correction. If a second oscillation starts, shake again. In the event of continued swinging, set down and start again at the taxi stage.

In the air, keep relaxed and remember to keep the ski tips up all the time. Dipping tips allows either the wind to catch the kite causing the body and kite to swing, or the loss of a ski (if this happens, drop the second ski and land without skis). At all times watch the observer and the horizon. Never look straight down as it affects equilibrium sensitivity.

Landing

Ski tips are kept up at all times while in the air and especially when approaching the water. Once on the water, ski as usual with the weight on the skis. (The throttle man will have to maintain a slow speed in order for the skier to do this.)

The observer will slow the boat down as the skier taxis to the dock area. When he starts to sink, the skier pushes the bar away and the observer pins him.

INTERMEDIATE FLYING

After taking several runs and getting the feel of flying and landing, the skier will want to learn how to control the kite and its actions to a larger degree.
Control of oscillation is the most important part of the novice's program. As the kite starts an oscillation (the kite swings out to one side, then back across to the other side and so on), one side of the trapeze bar drops below the other. This is the direction in which the oscillation moves.
The flyer moves his weight from the center of the trapeze to the low side and rides out the oscillation. As the kite approaches the top of the oscillation, the bar levels, and the weight of the body over the outside corner will prevent the kite from lowering its other side. In effect, what the flyer does is let the kite move out to one side and then hold it level, stiffling the return oscillation.

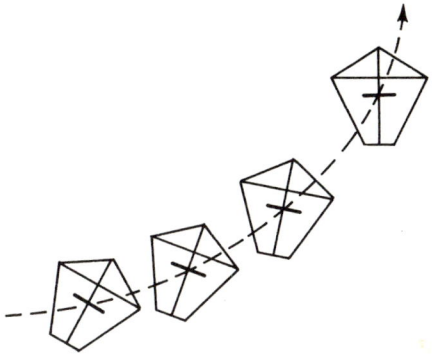

Trapeze bar during oscillation

Dry-land practice should precede attempts at oscillation control. All actions should be smooth and relaxed. Avoid "muscling" or jerking the kite down.
Weight shift from the center of the trapeze bar is one way of directing the kite (slaloming). Practice the weight shifts along the trapeze bar while taxiing. This results in slaloming the kite on the water using *only* weight placement in relation to the kite. Try coping with varied wind directions while taxiing and reacting with body position along the trapeze to control the kite.

Make any necessary adjustments to the harness before leaving the water. If it is necessary to turn, put the weight on the corner which is closest to the direction from which the wind is blowing (windward corner).

When set, signal the pinman and take off. Control the kite with the relaxed natural movements along the trapeze practiced earlier. Let the harness bear the weight. Do not muscle the kite.

As in taxiing, the skier can slalom the kite while airborne. The key is the same body position used before. A shift to the low corner of the bar causes an accelerated movement in that direction.

At the upper point of the oscillation (that point where the bar comes level), shift to the opposite end. This causes a resultant move down and across to the other side where another shift in weight causes the kite to fly back.

Experience and experimentation will enhance kiting skills to the point where the flyer will want to take part in one of the tournaments sponsored by a national kite flying association or a local group. A good instructor will be of value here.

The novice flyer should concentrate on relaxed moves and safety. With care and with teamwork between observer-pinman, driver, and flyer, the experience will be enjoyable and accident free.

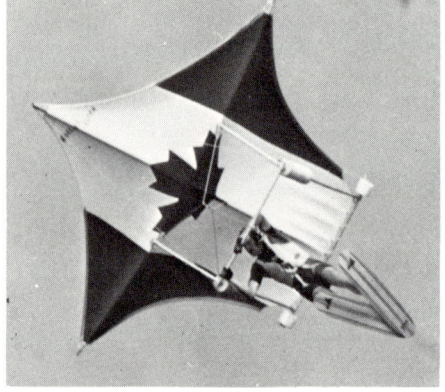

ADVANCED FLYING

As kiting expertise is developed, the flyer will want to attempt some more advanced moves while airborne. When tricking on a kite, make the moves complete, smooth and definite. Slow moves often result in a dunking for both flyer and kite.

Some tricks can be done with or without skis. Since tricks requiring skis are few in number, flyers who intend to trick should drop both skis. The pinman should remember exactly where the kiter has dropped his skis and retrieve them later if no pick-up boat is available.

Establishment of a kite frame or a high bar on land will allow the flyer adequate practice to develop these tricks.

180° Turn

The flyer starts from the normal front position, with the trapeze bar at eye level. Both hands are on the bar and spread wide apart. Weight is maintained by the harness fastened to the midpoint of the trapeze. The flyer should be in a stable position 10 to 25 feet above the water.

Remove the left hand from the bar, pass it under the bar on the boat side of the harness and place it in reverse position beside the right hand. Lean the head back and duck under the bar on the left side (where the hand was) while moving the right hand to the opposite corner of the bar. Let the harness bear the weight, not the arms.

The flyer is now flying backwards in a position which is the reverse of the normal. Flying backwards must be practiced by the flyer.

Control of oscillations when skiing backwards is the same as when skiing forwards. As the kite starts to move, shift the weight to the low side of the bar and ride out the oscillation. Keep the bar level at the crest or peak of the oscillation. Once stable, return to the front flying position.

The back position is also the safest and easiest for landing a flyer without skis. The backwards flyer is pinned about 5 to 8 feet above the water and the kite acts as an air brake. The flyer drops gently into the water.

360° Turn

After learning the 180° turn to both directions and back, the flyer may learn the 360° turn. As in a 360° turn on the water, first do a 180° turn, pause, and continue on around. Keep one hand on the trapeze when reaching under the bar and around the harness to the other side. This applies when the flyer is going from front-to-back or back-to-front.

In competition, the body must turn without pause through the 360°. The trunk must be straight and the legs must be horizontal. Maintain form through the learning series.

360° Free Turn

After a 360° turn the harness will be twisted. One way to remove the twist is to do a 360° free turn. To do this, initiate a slight spin, remove the hands completely from the trapeze, and place them at your sides. The body, in a semi-horizontal position, spins around a full 360° to the forward position.

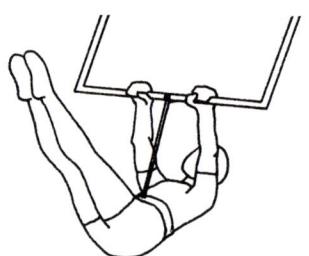

Body Swings—Front or Back

The body swing is the first trick in which the skis must be dropped. Slide the hand down the trapeze towards the point where the harness is fixed. Swing the body (cocked at the waist, with legs and feet together) up until the feet are at the same level as the trapeze bar. The body swing can be done either from the front or back skiing position. Abdominal control is necessary for this trick.

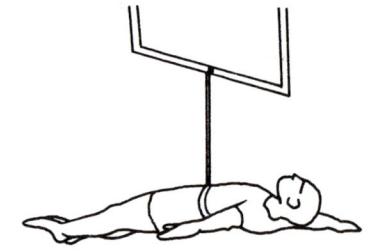

Free Layout—Front or Back

Starting either from the back or front position, arch the back and lie back until arms are straight with hands holding on to the trapeze bar. When the kite is stable, release the bar and hold the arms outstretched. The back is arched and the neck hyperextended. The body should be parallel to water surface.

The tricker may execute this trick directly from any of a number of other positions. In this way, sequences of tricks can be planned.

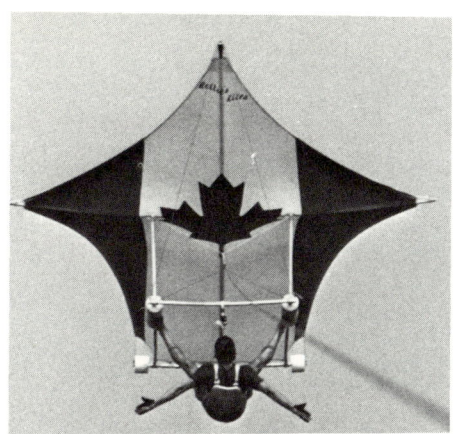

Free Front/Free Back Hold Layout

Again, this trick is done from either the front or back flying position. Cock the body at the waist and place the feet firmly against the rollers on the side bars or the bridles.

With the kite stabilized in flight, release the trapeze with both hands, lie back and extend the arms.

Hand Phalange Front

From either the front or back flying position, swing the feet back and straight up as you pull in on the bar.

The feet, in back phalange, can be run along the sail until they reach the bar behind the sail or rest on the sail immediately above the trapeze. Arms must be used to control the kite while the body is inverted.

Several continuations of this trick can be done. These include the inverted front or back phalange or free phalange, front or back.

Bar Roll

The roll over the bar is an off-shoot of the phalange. Swing the legs back and up and initiate a strong pull up with the arms. They have been pulled in closer to the center of the bar for added strength.

Initially, tuck the legs to facilitate the roll around the center of the bar and avoid the bridles of the kite. In a later stage of learning, straighten the legs and run the feet along the sail until over. Eventually a flyer will be able to perform the trick with legs relatively straight and without touching the sail.

It is important to complete the roll without pauses.

Bar Swan Front

The easiest way to get into a bar swan is to roll, stopping one-half the way through the roll and balancing on the bar at the waist or the stomach.

Straighten the body and legs, arch the back, hyperextend the neck and outstretch the arms sideways.

Front Press Layout

Initiate this trick from the front skiing position.
Place the feet on the float bars after securing the trapeze across the stomach.
Once the kite is stable, extend the arms out in push fashion.

Bailout

While it is not a recognized trick for competition, the bailout can be a spectacular finale to a ski show kite run. To do this, hook the arm over the trapeze such that the bar passes under the armpit. Pull up with the free arm and simultaneously release the harness from the kite. Keep the arm over the bar until you are ready to drop down and control the kite with both hands. This requires sliding the trapeze up the arm to the hand. Be prepared for a rapid upshot of the kite once the arm is removed from the trapeze.

From the bare-arm position at about 20 to 25 feet, release both hands simultaneously as you swing forward gently. The kite is heading into the wind and going quite slowly. Enter the water with arms at the sides.

As soon as the flyer leaves the kite, it is pinned. As a consequence, the flyer must remain underwater for a few seconds until the kite lands.

There are numerous other tricks which can be done in the air. These include knee hangs, toe and heel hangs, and bar sets. For complete rules and descriptions of these tricks, as well as information about kiting competition, contact a local or national kite flying association.

Chapter 10   Show Skiing

One aspect of waterskiing which seems to capture the imagination of everyone is show skiing, which consists of performances or displays of skill staged by competent skiers. Much of the material which goes into a show has already been discussed throughout the book; items such as kite flying, barefooting, tricks and slalom skiing. Other aspects will be discussed here.

PADDLE SKIING

Skiing on a paddle has always been a favorite of ski enthusiasts and is a stunt which is very simple to execute.

Method One

Start in the water with the slalom ski on the wrong foot (the foot not normally slalomed on) and a canoe paddle inserted in the back of the flotation device. It is easily accessible to the skier on the water.

Once skiing, reach back and grasp the paddle, bring it around to the front, and point the handle towards the boat.

Remove the slalom foot from the back toepiece and place it on the blade of the paddle. Gradually, while still supporting the paddle with the hands, transfer the weight on to the paddle. Once eighty percent of the weight has been transferred on to the paddle, and it is stable, remove the hand and simply drop the ski.

Place the free foot on the ski behind the other one, as in slalom skiing, and control the ski in the same manner.

Leaning back increases the spray and enhances the act.
To initiate the trick, the speed of the boat is approximately that used in beginner barefooting, or 2 to 3 mph slower.
The trick may be done either inside or outside the wake, depending on water conditions prevalent in the area.

Method Two

There is a second method for getting up on a paddle. Start in the water with the normal slalom foot on the paddle blade and the other foot in a normal ski. The rope must be taut to keep the paddle from slipping away while the skier is getting up on the surface. Place the paddle under the foot such that the handle is pointing away from the boat. Once up, it is a simple matter to drop the ski and place the free foot on the paddle. With the paddle in this position, many skiers find there is more control of movement from side to side because of the rudder or keel effect of the handle in the water. It is, however, not as showy a method and therefore is usually replaced by the first method for ski shows.

Numerous variations of paddle skiing can be devised. One such modification is toehold paddle skiing. It is achieved in much the same manner as normal toehold tricks.

SHOE SKIS

Another ski show favorite is skiing on shoe skis, which are shortened skis approximately 15 to 17 inches in length and mounted with normal pairs bindings. Shoe skis are very simple to ski on, despite giving the appearance of great difficulty.

The boat speed is the same as for paddle skiing but the method used in getting up differs.

There are several easy methods for getting up, although some may display more showmanship.

Method One

If a starter ski is not available, the skier gets up on the disc. Sit on the back half of the disc with the shoe skis on and feet, a little more than shoulder width apart, hanging over the front edge. This keeps the front of the disc out of the water while the boat starts up. Signal the driver when ready for the boat to accelerate.

When the boat achieves desired speed the disc starts to plane. To get up, gradually transfer weight from the back of the disc to the shoe skis.

The disc falls behind. From here, it is like skiing on ordinary pairs.

Sit down in the water to stop.

Method Two

The disc is also used in this method of starting shoe skiers, but this time the skier stands towards the rear of the disc as the boat attains speed.

He simply hops off and plants the back of the shoe skis in the water.

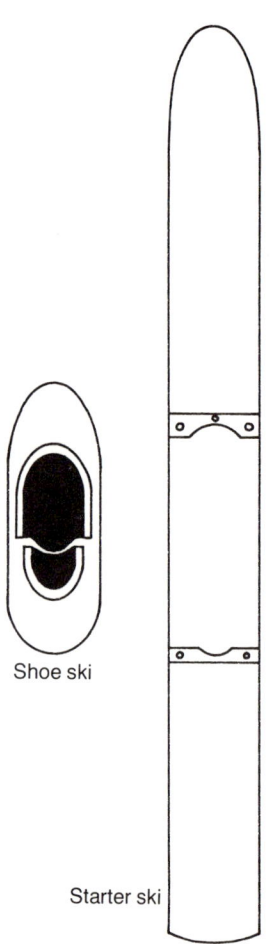

Shoe ski

Starter ski

Alternate methods which might be implemented in ski shows include using a starter ski, jump starting off the dock on to the disc and then on to the water, or starting off the dock. All are equally exciting for the show ski viewer.

Most of the tricks done on ordinary trick skis can be added to the shoe skier's repertoire. Seeing a shoe skier doing 180s, 360s, and wake turns can be extremely exciting for the viewers of a ski show.

SKIER'S SALUTE

A popular way to open the show is with the skier's salute. This is usually done by some girls carrying flags or penants, and any number of skiers can take part.

On normal skis, the skiers pass by the dock or viewing area and raise one ski such that it is at right angles to the surface of the water. All the skiers should raise the same leg at the same time and lower the leg at the same time. Usually two passes are made at the start of a show.

TANDEM

Another favourite is the tandem act, which features a male and a female skier working together to perform a number of configurations on skis. This requires a little more practice.

The hardest step is the mount by the woman following dropping of the skis. It can, however, be mastered with some practice.

The two skiers go out with even length ropes and ski side by side behind the boat.

The woman drops her outside ski and places her foot in the man's hand. She transfers her weight to that foot while she places her arm around the man's shoulder and exerts pressure there.

When her weight is transferred, she quickly drops her other ski and swings her leg up and over the shoulder of the man.

Once she is sitting on the man's shoulders, the woman drops the rope (over his rope) so that it can be pulled in by the observer.

From this position, the woman can execute a number of beautiful formations with her male counterpart's assistance.

For instance, the woman may hook her leg under the arm of the male and simply lie backwards while gracefully spreading her arms.

If the man assumes a squat position, the woman can stand on his thighs. He gives her additional support by holding her knees.

Getting down from a tandem act is easily accomplished by the woman dropping down on to the front of the skis and resting her weight on the man's body. She rides inside his arms and lets him control the skis.

When doing tandem:
- Talk to each other throughout the act and keep each other informed.
- Practice each facet of the act on dry land. Make sure it is perfected on land before going out and doing it in the water.
- Make sure the boat driver is competent and knows each part of the act.

113

PYRAMID

A spectacular act in any ski show is the pyramid act which features a number of women on the shoulders of some supporting men.

The key to any pyramid is in the building. A three-person pyramid is used for demonstration purposes. Other number combinations (e.g., five people, seven people) may be used.

The three skiers come together, with the person who will be the top of the pyramid in the center and the two base people flanking her.

The woman drops a ski and places her free foot on the thigh of one of the squatting base people while her other arm goes around the shoulder of the other person. The men on the bottom have interlocked arms to provide the woman with support and to ensure that the skiers on the bottom do not split apart.

In the second stage, the woman drops her remaining ski, places that foot on the thigh of the other base man and stands up. The men keep their arms interlocked throughout the act.

In the third step, the woman steps up to one man's shoulder while she maintains her grip on her towline and the thigh of the other base person.

Finally, the woman is positioned on both shoulders of her supporting skiers and she is in a stable position where she can wave to the crowd, hold flags or do anything which might add to the image created by the act.

In building, have the rope of the top skier about 12 inches longer than the other two ropes. Both of the men on the bottom should be strong skiers of approximately the same height. Their thighs should be free of attire which might slip as the climber exerts pressure upon them.

When building with more than three people, one side of the pyramid is constructed first and then the other.

Getting down from the pyramid should be made as exciting as the act itself. Such finales as having the top party back flip off the pyramid are effective. Use your imagination.

DISC AND CHAIR

Another act which will add to the enjoyment of the crowd is the one in which the skier uses a disc or the combination of disc and chair or disc and ladder.

Many of the tricks done on a pair of skis can also be performed on the disc. A pass doing a routine of these can be finished with the skier performing a handstand while skiing on the chair and disc.

Obviously this trick needs practice both on and off the water. Note that the handle is tied to the chair, which has been thrown into the water from the boat.

Use your imagination to make this either an exciting or a comical act in a ski show.

AROUND THE BOAT

There are two versions of this trick. It can be done with a slalom ski and a normal length rope (75 feet), or with trick skis and a trick rope (35 feet). In either case, an essential piece of equipment is a pylon with a high enough point of attachment for the rope to move over the boat from stern to bow during the trick. In actual fact, the boat moves under the taut rope when it makes the sharp turn.

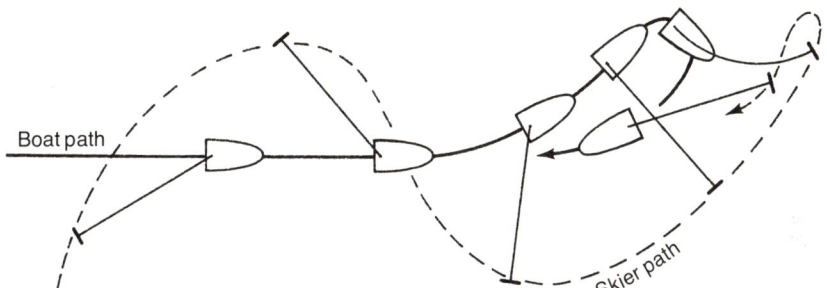

Trick Skier's Version

This trick can be done with a trick rope and a boat capable of making a very sharp turn (one with a narrow turning circle). The boat moves at about 22 to 23 mph at the start of the trick. On the whip, a speed of 30 mph is achieved. Because a skier on trick skis can stay on the surface for a longer period of time than a skier on a slalom ski, this trick does not have to be as rushed as the slalom ski version.

Slalom Version

The boat should be moving at about 35 mph at the start of the turn.
Start from the right side of the boat in a position outside the wake.
Swing across the left side of the boat to a position as far as possible outside of the wake.
Cut toward the right side of the boat. The boat driver steers the boat slightly to the left. This causes the skier to be moving at about 50 to 55 mph because of the *crack the whip* effect of the turning boat.
The skier is at his peak velocity as he reaches the termination of his swing outside the wake at the right of the boat. The boat driver cuts back on the throttle and makes a hard turn to the right.
The boat is in the middle of the sharp turn, and the towrope moves over the bow of the boat.
The boat driver completes the sharp turn, and the rope is once again in the normal position off the stern of the boat. The boat driver must increase the speed of the boat to prevent the skier from sinking. The skier may have to adjust his position to face the boat as it moves off on its new course.
The success of this trick depends on the rope being kept taut. The boat driver achieves this by proper boat speed and by his sharp steering in the turn.

CLOWN ACT

One act that should be included in any ski show is the clown act. It is comic relief, and anything which will entertain people and make them laugh can be used. The clown act should reflect personal capabilities. Humorous costumes can be worn to dress up the act, and loud communication between the skiers and all the parties involved in the show should be heard at all times.

Anything done on the water is acceptable. This includes *apparent* out of control skiing, wake jumps, collisions, and utilization of the jump and/or other boats. Extreme caution must be exercised at all times.

The clown act can be the main event of the show and can certainly enhance all performances.

ANNOUNCING

It has been stated many times that the announcer either makes or breaks a ski show. A good announcer announces each act as if it is the first time he has seen it. He becomes involved in the show, dramatizes every event, and actually becomes a part of each act.

His knowledge of the sport is extensive and he has at his finger tips information about each facet of the sport. He can use this information to fill time if the need arises.

A good announcer succeeds in building the audience to a climax in especially daring events in the show. He relates the audience to each act.

As well as being fully knowledgable about the skiing, the announcer knows each skier and has a wealth of knowledge available about each of them. If the announcer makes the viewers feel personally related to those on the water, it enhances their enjoyment of the spectacle.

Good announcers in waterski shows tie the show together by giving it continuity from act to act, by filling the gaps with information, and by making those watching feel a part of it all. The announcer is truly the mainstay in the successful ski show.

PICK-UP BOATS

Another important facet of the ski show is the pickup boat and its crew. The crew must be familiar with the entire show. They know where to retrieve dropped skis or skiers and are skilled first-aid people.

All too often these people are overlooked, and anyone is put in the pickup boat. The result may be an enthusiastic driver scurrying to get into position to pick up the dropped skis in a barefoot act and, in so doing, causing waves which spoil the entire act. This can be averted by carefully selecting a crew.

GENERAL POINTERS

The following pointers will help establish a successful ski show:

- Make sure all people are familiar with the schedule for the ski show. Adequate printed act lists complete with information concerning the act, personnel involved, boats involved, and equipment should be distributed to all participants, especially the announcer, dock manager and boat drivers.
- One person should take charge of all the dock activities. Also, he makes sure that all equipment is out before the show and all is returned after it.

- Have each skier make sure that his equipment is laid out and that he knows where it is at all times.
- Care should be taken to make sure that the ropes are always ready and kept free from knots. Any shortened or lengthened rope should also be ready before the show.
- Immediately before the show, run over all events with the participants to make sure that all is ready.
- Keep things moving throughout the show. Avoid lags between acts. If someone is having a bad day, don't pull him up for a fourth time. Leave him and proceed to the next act. The announcer can cover for it.

A good idea is to have everyone work together on the dock to make sure that the next act is always ready and waiting.

- Make the show as professional as possible by avoiding petty or boring acts. Make it fluid.
- Work together.

The following is a list of acts which can be included in a ski show. A show can range anywhere from one hour to one hour and forty-five minutes.

Of course, many of these acts will not be possible for an initial production, but the list provides a guide of what can be done. Outline the ski show carefully so that no one person is responsible for two acts in a row or for an overly demanding amount of work in the show. Substitute acts which are within the skier's level of experience. It detracts from the show if acts are not done well.

Act	Description
1	Skiers salute with two passes; first pass with flags, second pass with legs raised and skiers waving to the fans.
2	Paddle skiing; two passes with the second one toehold.
3	Tandem act; up to three passes.
4	Flat kite or double flat kite; several passes one slalom, two tricks.
5	Slalom ski; two passes.
6	Jumping; three jumps illustrating the different phases in learning how to jump (could substitute double or triple jumping with crosses over and under).
7	Around the boat.
8	Clown act; several passes, could use any equipment including jump, dock and kites.
9	Trapeze on a delta kite; two passes featuring a girl and a guy doing tricks on a delta kite.
10	Trick run; two to three passes possibly, with a back start in deep water if the area permits.
11	Shoe skis; two passes.
12	Pyramid; one pass.
13	Barefoot run; one to two passes if possible.
14	Clown act; slightly shorter than before and of a different nature.
15	Delta flight; one free flight from 500 to 1000 feet.
16	Applause and bows on the dock; invite to return.

Music

Music is an asset to any ski show. It attracts people before the show and provides a relaxed background atmosphere throughout. Play either popular music or instrumental march music, if possible.

Chapter 11 Conditioning

The purpose of this chapter is to acquaint the skier with some specific exercises which will prepare him for a greater participation in and enjoyment of this sport.

These are by no means the only exercises or ways to get conditioned for waterskiing, but they represent the type of program necessary to help improve skier strength and endurance.

When designing a training program, several factors determine its nature. Examination of the following will help the skier plan a conditioning program for himself.

- Implementation of any exercise in a program must be skill task specific. That is, any exercise should work the muscles through the motions utilized in the movement pattern which will be used in the water. Specific exercises develop those muscles which need development for a defined purpose. An exercise is of maximum benefit only when this is achieved.

- Waterskiing is a sport demanding strength and endurance. Hence any program should incorporate exercises designed to develop muscular strength and endurance, as well as cardiorespiratory capacities.

- The skier should examine his own strengths and weaknesses and design a program that focuses on eliminating the weaknesses and improving the strengths.

- The skier should examine his skiing technique and isolate those muscles or muscle groups which need to be exercised. Any exercises should be tailored to improve performance in these muscles.

It has been suggested that the only real way to improve the strength and endurance capacities of the water skier is to have him ski continuously, to the point of exhaustion. This is a foolish training system. Although somewhat beneficial in conditioning, it can be very harmful in causing the development and practice of bad habits for the skier. These are hard to correct later. In addition, this type of training is expensive from a time loss point of view. A much more efficient and rewarding system can be implemented by the waterskier.

The following recommended exercises should prove very beneficial in preparing for the skiing season.

WEIGHT TRAINING

The purpose of weight training is to minimize increases in body bulk while maximizing increases in strength and endurance. Use of a number of sets of weights with light to moderate training poundages produces increases in endurance capacities of muscles, whereas exercises employing heavy poundage increase the strength or power capabilities of the muscles worked. A compromise situation must be established to provide for equal gains in strength and endurance.

Such a program usually uses four sets (each exercise is done 4 times) decreasing the number of repetitions (reps) each time while increasing the poundage. An exercise employing such a system follows:
10 reps at 50 pounds
8 reps at 55 pounds
6 reps at 60 pounds
4 reps at 65 pounds
In increasing poundage, a good rule to establish is to add 5 pounds to each level when the skier can easily move the specified poundage through the number of repetitions, plus one or two more. This is a guideline which varies from person to person.

SPECIFIC EXERCISES

Thigh Extensions

A leg table will be necessary for this exercise. Thigh extensions develop the musculature surrounding the knees and strengthens the extensors. This is invaluable in jumping, where the knees have tremendous stress exerted on them both on the jump and on the landings.

Sit on the table with back straight, head up and hands flat on the table. Place weights on the system so that it is possible to do only 15 reps. Raise the leg slowly placing the stress on the upper leg. Do not cheat. The tendency here is to jerk the weight up with the assistance of the upper body.

Raise the weight slowly to the fully extended position. Next, lower the leg to the starting position slowly. Use the weight's resistance in lowering for full benefit from the exercise. Example:
Repeat 15 times with maximum weight
Repeat 10 times with maximum weight + 5 pounds
Repeat 8 times with maximum weight + 10 pounds
Repeat 6 times with maximum weight + 15 pounds.

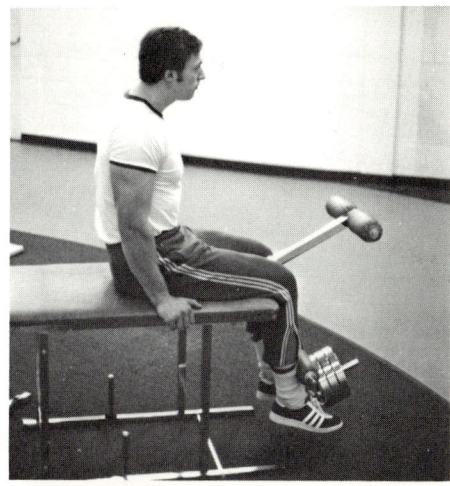

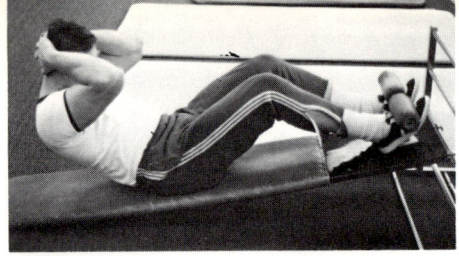

Incline Situps

Use of an abdominal or incline board greatly accelerates the development of the stomach or abdominal muscles. Basically, an ordinary board 10 feet by 2 feet with a strap under which to place one's feet will suffice. In addition to working the abdominal muscles, bent-leg incline situps can increase strength in the lower back muscles.

From the prone position, with feet hooked under the strap, heels close to the butt, and hands clasped behind the head, sit up slowly and smoothly (no jerking). Exhale as you sit up. Stop at the position where the chest touches the knees.

Return to the starting position, inhaling as you slowly lie down. Work the muscles as you return. Don't just flop back.

The exercise is more effective if a weight plate or dumbbell is held behind the head. This adds to the resistance offered the muscle. At least 25 reps should be done per set. Weight is added each time.

4 sets of 25 reps.

Add 5 to 10 pounds when 25 reps can be done easily and correctly.

Regular Barbell Curls

This exercise can be done either using a two-hand curl or using a pair of dumbbells for individual curls. Use of individual dumbbells is assumed to be better as it more closely approximates those moments at which the skier is pulling in with one hand during a slalom run. Both exercises, however, develop an essential muscle for the skier, the biceps. They also work the other muscles of the forearm, the upper arm and the shoulder region.

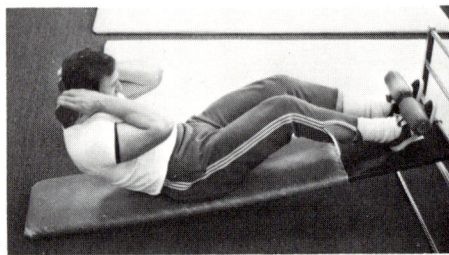
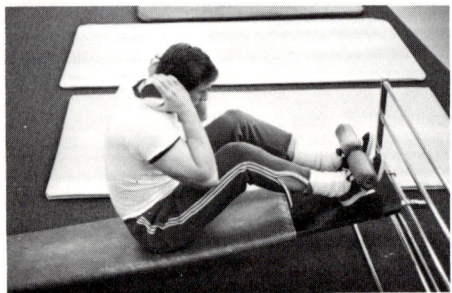

With elbows at the sides, grasp the barbell (or dumbbells) with a palms up grip and fully extend the arms downwards to the sides.

Without jerking, and keeping the elbows at the sides, "curl" the bar slowly up while inhaling.

The bar should reach the shoulders and is then lowered to the original position. The lowering of the bar should be slow and steady, resisting the movement downwards as it were. Exhale during the down motion.

Start with a weight which can be handled comfortably for 10 reps. Work up to 15 reps and add 5 pounds. Do 4 sets as before:
10 reps with 10 pounds
8 reps with 15 pounds
6 reps with 20 pounds
4 reps with 25 pounds

Reverse Barbell Curls

Reverse curls, while having an effect on the same areas of the upper arm, tend to develop to a greater extent the forearms and wrist areas. This is essential for the waterskier in maintaining his control over the rope.

The action is a duplicate of the above.

Elbows are at the sides, head up, back straight. However, this time the bar is grasped in a different manner. The hands are placed fairly wide apart in the palms down position (the reverse of the previous hand position for the curl).

Curl the bar slowly up to the shoulders. Complete the action slowly and deliberately. Lower to the start position, resisting the downward movement. Repetition of sets should be as in the regular curls pattern.

Quarter Squats/Half Squats

Squats are an important part of any weight training program and especially in a program for a skier. This exercise is designed to strengthen the quadriceps, the muscles of the upper leg. Strengthening this area is necessitated by pressures exerted on the legs during jumping—either in the landing or by the intense pressure of the jump ramp itself.

Squats can be done either with or without a 2 inch by 4 inch board under the heels. Its presence removes some of the pressure on the lower back during the exercise. Start by standing with the legs shoulder width apart and arms stretched back to hold the weights in place. It is a good idea to insert a towel between the bar and the neck for comfort.

Keeping the back straight and the head up, and maintaining a wide grasp, lower yourself by bending the knees.

The low point for the quarter squats.

The low point for the half squats.

Return to the up position.
Three to four sets of 10 repetitions should be done. Start with a weight that can be handled comfortably for 10 reps. Add 10 pounds and do 10 reps, 10 pounds more and do 8 reps, 10 pounds more and do 6 reps.

Pulley Rows

This exercise is most beneficial when it is as specific as possible. If it is done standing, the feet are placed as a slalom skier's would be. Whether it is done standing or sitting, the pull is made to the hip, hence developing the muscles specific to the task.

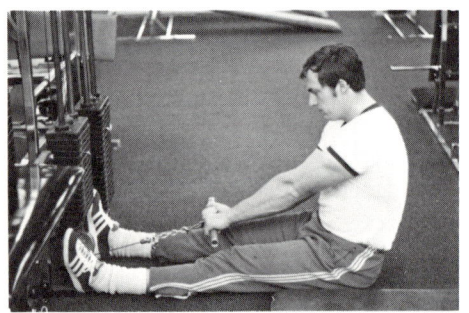

A ski handle and wall pulley are an asset in achieving increased pull power needed in both slalom and jumping.

Sitting pulley rows feature a pull to the hip region of the skier. Slight body rotation is observed here.

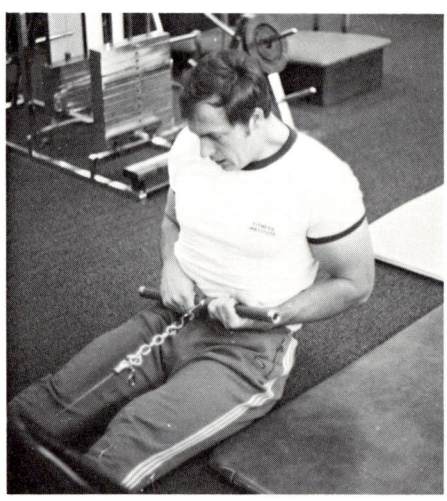

The grip is the baseball grip characteristic of slalom and jump skiers. It is a more natural and powerful grip for pulling than the palms down grip.

 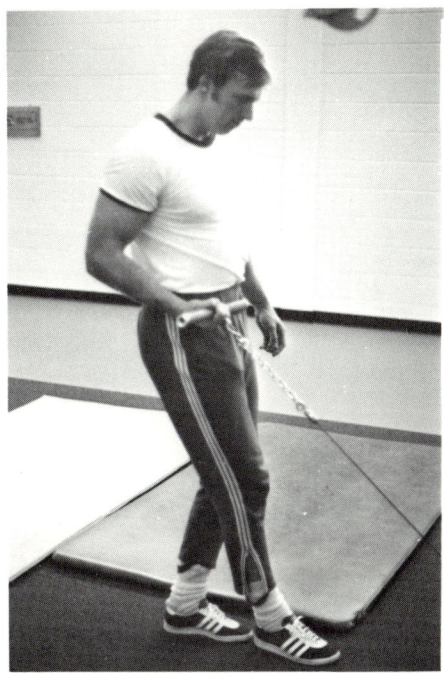

Standing pulley rows are done with the back straight and feet positioned in slalom ski fashion. The rope pull is to the hip and the baseball grip is used. For best results, alternate the hip to which the rope is pulled.

Working again with the maximum weight at which you can do 10 reps in strict form, work up to 15 reps on the first set. As before, add 5 to 10 pounds on each set and decrease reps by two.

Do 4 sets:
12 reps with maximum weight
10 reps with maximum weight + 5-10 pounds
8 reps with maximum weight + 10-20 pounds
6 reps with maximum weight + 15-30 pounds

Behind the Neck Presses

The shoulders are an area subjected to varied strains ranging from pressures of slalom or jumping to the angulation changes in the pull of the trick skier. Additional work must be done to accommodate the shoulder to such stress. If done properly, behind the neck presses are one of the best exercises for strengthening the shoulder region.

Hold the bar over the head. Arms extend straight up, palms face the front and the head is up. Inhale as you commence the exercise.

Inhale as you lower. Do not allow the arms to move forward. Bend the arms at the elbows while lowering the weight.

In the down position, note the position of the upper arm and head.

Exhale as you return to the *up* or start position. Retain the straight up position of the forearms. Do not cheat by allowing them to jerk forward. Start with a weight which you can handle for 10 reps. When you've worked up to 15 reps then add an extra 5 pounds and start at 10 reps again.

10 reps with maximum weight
8 reps with maximum weight + 5 pounds
6 reps with maximum weight + 10 pounds
4 reps with maximum weight + 15 pounds

Good Morning Exercise

In trick skiing, control of the body is of key importance in establishing balance or equilibrium positions. Hence, abdominal control is desirable. The good morning exercise strengthens the abdominal muscles and the back muscles.

The barbell is placed behind the neck and is held as in the squat position. The start position is standing erect.

The body is bent forward at the waist, and the head is kept such that you can look forward.

The back, in the down position, should be parallel to the ground.
This, as well as the situps, can be done with varied weights daily. Care should be taken to begin with light weights so as to avoid back strain. Repetitions should range from 10 to 25 per set.

Bent Rowing

Another exercise which develops the skier's pulling power and strengthens his back muscles is bent rowing. To develop both endurance and power, use 3 to 4 sets, starting with 10 to 15 reps and working down to 4 reps with heavy weight.

With the back parallel to the floor and the head up, start with arms extended and grasp the barbell. The weight of the barbell should allow you to do 10 reps. Inhale as you draw the weight upwards slowly.

In the up position, the back is straight, the elbows are up, and the eyes are looking ahead. From this position, slowly lower the weight. Resist the urge to drop it.

When weight training, have an adequate warm-up before each session. There should be three sessions per week.

ISOMETRIC EXERCISES

These exercises are done after weight training exercises. Portions of the waterskiing act are considered to be isometric in nature. There is great force exerted on the muscle, resulting in *static contraction,* or contraction without a change in the length of the muscle. Isometric exercises cause such contraction. This contraction occurs when the person exerts a force against an immovable object. Such exercises are useful for the waterskier.

Incorporating isometric body contraction in the weight workout will add to total body muscle tone and power.

Other types of isometrics can be developed for waterskiers. Generally, however, the weight training will be more beneficial. Listed below are several other typical isometrics.

Using a power rack, a bar affixed between two vertical poles so that it can't move upwards and providing maximum resistance, assume the slalom ski stance beneath the bar. With your feet correctly placed, the bar across the neck, and hands in the squat position, inhale and exert total body pressure upwards. Hold the muscles in isometric contraction for 15 seconds and relax for several minutes. Repeat 2 or 3 times per workout.

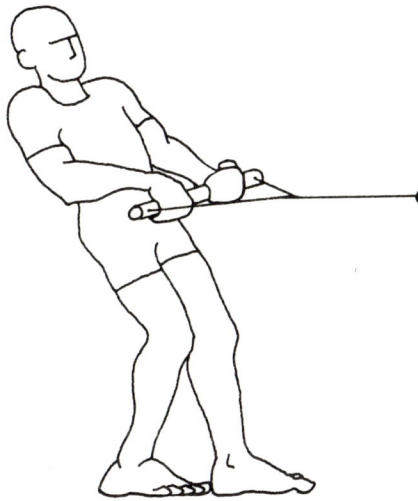

A rope is fastened to a wall or some other immobile object. Standing in the slalom position, pull as when running a slalom course. Pull in low to the hip.

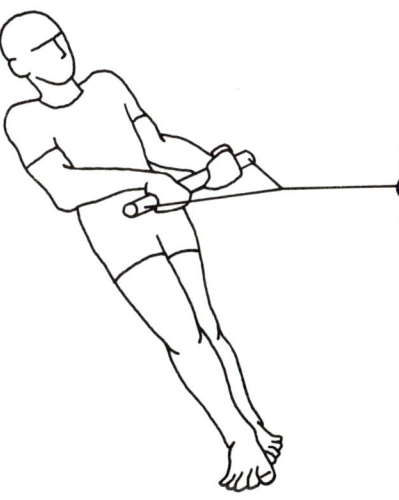

Standing as if pulling for a jumping double wake cut, lean and pull as hard as possible for 5 to 10 seconds. Again, pull low.

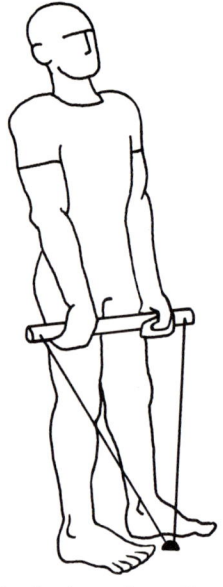

The rope is fastened to the floor in front of your feet. Lean back and pull upwards, keeping the feet parallel and arms straight and close into the body.

Hook the feet under a sofa or some such object and attempt to raise the legs. Keep them straight.
In the same position, but with knees bent, attempt to raise the feet.
Hold each contraction for 5 to 8 seconds. Repeat up to 5 contractions per workout. Rest one minute between each contraction. Concentrate all the while you are working out with isometrics. Always breathe out slightly when exerting maximum efforts with isometrics.

Workouts should be done three times per week (e.g. Monday, Wednesday and Friday). The following is a suggested sequence (variations depend upon the person and his strengths and weaknesses).
Monday, Friday
1) Squats
2) Sit-ups
3) Bent Rows
4) Reverse Curls
5) Pully Rows
Wednesday
1) Knee Extensions
2) Good Morning Exercises
3) Sit-ups
4) Regular Curls
5) Press
6) Isometrics

OTHER EXERCISES

Though not necessarily proven, other training programs could be implemented by the skier to improve his performance, and hence his enjoyment of the sport.

Running

Running improves leg muscle tone as well as cardiorespiratory endurance.

Swimming

This is an excellent conditioning activity for the skier, which results in cardiovascular improvement.

Trampoline

Working out on a trampoline improves cardiorespiratory fitness. It could also be utilized through turns, flips and rotations to develop a sense of equilibrium in other than normal positions such as those which occur in trick skiing.

Gymnastics

This provides an excellent form of conditioning as well as an opportunity for the skier to develop his kinesthetic sense. This sense informs a person of the position of all his body's parts in relation to each other and space. It is especially beneficial for either trick skiers or jumpers.

These are not the only programs which can be implemented. However, any exercise should be specific to the skills involved in the sport. The muscle is worked through the same range and pattern of motion as in the skiing skill.

Chapter 12   Ski Equipment Maintenance

IN-SEASON CARE

Once the skier has selected his equipment, he has usually invested a fair amount of money and he should protect this investment by prolonging the life of his equipment through constant care and maintenance, especially during the ski season. Some suggestions are made here to help in equipment maintenance.

Boats

Every morning, before the first ski run, it is a good idea to allow about fifteen minutes to do some work on the boat. Dew on the top of the boat and seats is chamoised or dried off, and the interior is cleaned out. The main reason for this is neatness, but it also aids in boat life and skiing safety. The bottom of the boat is scrubbed off twice a week with a stiff scrub brush. This removes most of the algae or scum which forms on boats in water. Large amounts of algae when allowed to build up can slow a recreational skier's boat by several miles per hour. This is critical if the boat's maximum speed is 36 mph. If the boat is kept neat and clean throughout the skiing season, skiing will be much more enjoyable, boat speed and performance will be improved greatly, and chances of accidents will be reduced.

Skis

Care of the skis during the season is critical. At the end of each day, skis are inspected for nicks in the wood or fiberglass. These chips are sanded down to remove any extruding slivers, and the skis are allowed to dry. If the nick is in wood skis, plastic wood (marine quality) or epoxy (2 in 1) can be used to fill it before a coat of good quality urethane or polyurethane is applied. This acts as a sealer and prevents water from entering the wood. Water allowed to attack the wood will result in grains lifting, discolorations in the wood, waterlogging or even warping. If the skis are fiberglass, a good epoxy filler should be used.

Special attention should be paid to trick skis which have been used by beginners. Frequently the edges are badly marked by chips or nicks. These must be seen to immediately. Jump skis are also susceptible to damage from makeshift jumps which may have nails protruding from the ramp surface. Jump skis should be patched and immediately urethaned. Many of the fiberglass jump or trick skis have rubber edges which protect the ski edges.

Common sense dictates other rules of ski care during the season. Exposure of rubber to the sun results in cracked and rotting bindings, and exposure of some skis to extreme weather conditions can cause damage. Hence, protect skis by turning them away from the sun so the bindings are shaded, or insert them in protective ski bags. Skis should be carried in ski bags if you travel regularly with them.

Special care should be taken of slalom ski keels. Do not stand in the ski on the dock and avoid putting the keel in the slot between dock boards as both of these will lead to bent keels and impairment of skiing.

The best way to care for skis at the waterfront is to construct a ski rack and fasten it to the dock. A simple rack can be made by nailing two 2x4 boards about 30 inches apart. Each board is fitted with one-half inch wooden dowels every 6 inches or so. The skis can be inverted and placed on the dowels with the bindings turned away from the sun's rays.

Place a piece of indoor-outdoor carpet on the dock where the skiers land. This affords extra protection when the skier places his ski on the dock and averts chips or nicks.

Ropes

Ropes are the most frequently abused piece of equipment. They are often found mooring the boat at the dock or wrapped around some propeller. Ropes should be maintained as well as other equipment. Keep them free of knots, which cause weak spots in the line.

When coiling ropes make the coils long and even, about 18 to 24 inches, and turn the kinks out of the rope. Kinks are the forerunners of knots.

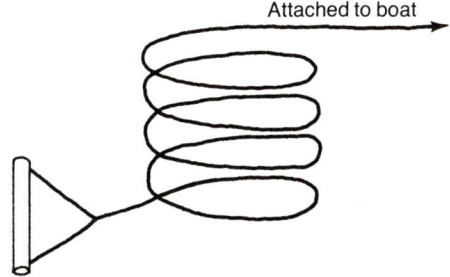

When letting the rope out for the skier, lay the coils on the water such that the end attached to the boat is uppermost. This enables the boat to idle out unreeling the line and decreases the probability of knots. Never throw the line out. Always lay it down.

Every skier should be adept at *splicing ropes.* This is a method of joining rope. Numerous types of splices are available to the skier, and several are described here. Practice these; they will save you money and time. It is economical for a skier who knows how to splice a ski line to make his own.

Lock splice

This splice is used for making loops for quick and reversable line joins and end loops of the rope. It is a simple splice to achieve.

- Seal off one end of the rope with a flame so that it is pointed and smooth, and insert into a fid if one is available.

- Make a loop with the pointed end (fid end) by inserting it through the strands and pulling it out the other side until the loop is the desired size.

- Take the fid end and re-enter the rope about one-half inch on the loop side of the first penetration. Work the tip down the center of the rope and bisect the first rope. This *locks* the rope at the desired loop size and makes it unnecessary to sew the join.

- Diamond braided rope works like a Chinese finger lock; the harder it is pulled, the harder it grasps. Conversely, if the rope is pushed together, it widens the diameter of the center core of the rope.
Using this principle, work the pointed or fid end down the center of the rope until the end length of rope is exhausted (it is all within the center core area). Remove the fid if one was used.

- Pull the rope tight to make the splice tight. There should be 6 to 8 inches in the *tail* of the completed splice section.

Eye splice

- Make a loop similar to that in the lock splice. Insert the tip and work it down the core of the diamond braid.

- Make sure there are at least 6 to 8 inches of tail in the core and the loop is the desired size.

- Remove fid.

- Hook the loop over the pylon and pull tight.

- Reinforce and lock the loop splice by sewing or stitching the completed splice with a heavy nylon thread.

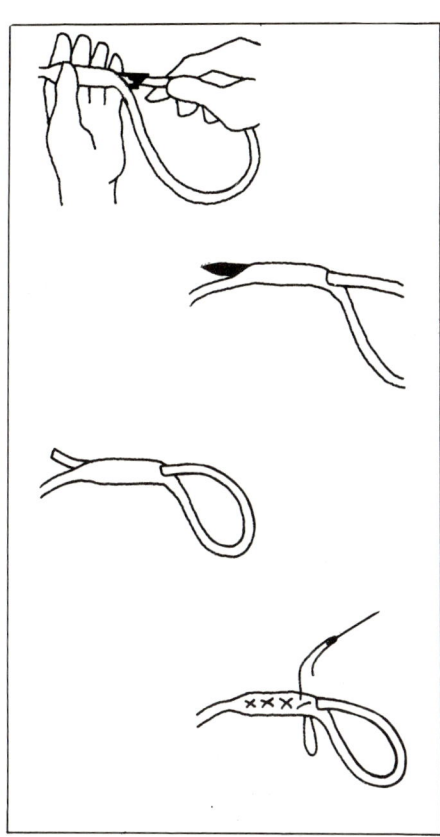

Tow Bar Splice

- Using 4-1/2 to 5 feet of rope from the spool, thread the sealed pointed end through the handle.
- With the 15 to 20 inches which is through the hole, eye splice a loop on the inside of the hole. Do this with both ends of the handle. This gives an exceedingly tight grasp which won't give way under pressure, as knots are prone to do.
- Pull the eye as tightly as possible against the handle, and stitch.
- Pull the spliced portion through the handle holes.
- Connect the handle portion with eye or lock splice at the end of the rope.

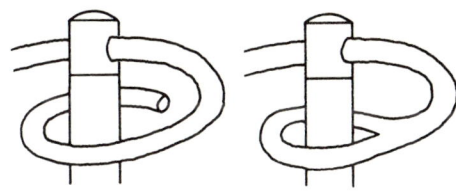

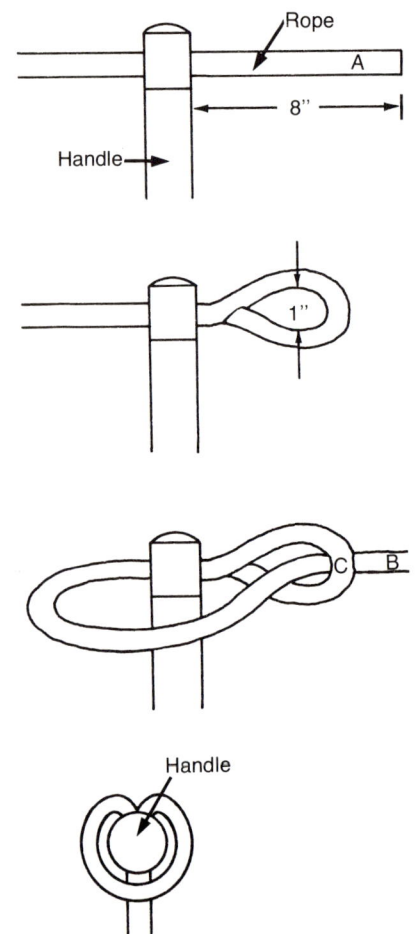

Bournes Splice

This splice was introduced by Mr. David Bournes of the Margesson Company Limited in Toronto. It has proven to be an extremely strong splice. The junction between the handle and the towrope will not move or slide and thus present the skier with a lopsided handle arrangement.

- Cut two lengths of rope—one approximately 40 inches in length, and the other roughly 96 inches.
- Using the 40-inch length first, pass one end through the hole in the handle such that 8 inches extends on the other side.
- Make an eye loop with this end (end A) approximately 1 inch across.
- Take the long end of the same rope (end B) and push it through the middle of the loop (going from inside to the outside) at point C.
- Roll the loop over the end of the tow bar.
- Pull the long end (B) and the loop until tight on the tow bar.
- Repeat this same procedure with the long (96-inch) piece of rope at the other end of the tow bar.

- To join the rope and the tow bar to the towline:
Take the 96-inch length (X) and pass the 40-inch length (Y) through the center of X, 10 to 12 inches from the handle. Adjust it such that both sides are equal as shown.
Follow the pattern established in diagrams.

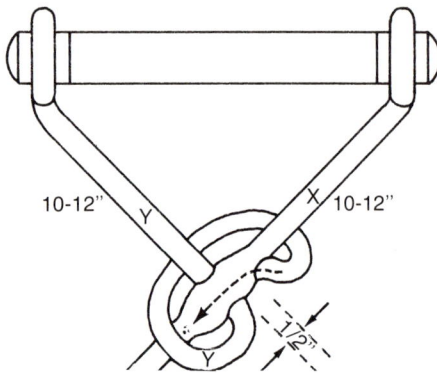

When Y is spliced into X, it also goes through itself

- At the other end of X make a similar loop or use the eye or lock splice described earlier.

POST-SEASON CONDITIONING

Boats

After the season has ended, the boat is thoroughly cleaned and prepared for winter storage. Algae and scum are removed from the exterior surface and a check for damage is made. Repairs should be attended to in the off-season.
The gas tank is emptied and the engine checked and tuned.

Skis

Ski storage during the off-season is as important as during the season. Examine the skis thoroughly for nicks, gouges, splitting wood, or any other damage.
In the case of wooden skis, it is a good idea to remove the hardware and sand the skis down lightly. Apply urethane or polyurethane and remount the bindings. Fiberglass skis should be examined as well and repaired with epoxy if necessary.
Skis are stored in protective ski bags in an area which is cool and dry. With thin, wide skis such as tricks, it is an excellent idea to use a press to ensure maintenance of the rocker design.

Ropes

Coil the ropes with care, avoiding kinks and knots, and store with the skis.
All equipment is an expensive proposition and should be treated with care. Maintaining the equipment will lengthen its period of usefulness.